woulda.
coulda.
shoulda.

*A divorce coach's guide
to staying married*

HOLD THE BULLS#!T

Jennifer Hurvitz

ISBN: 978-1-7336158-2-2

Edited by: Amy Ashby

Published by Warren Publishing
Charlotte, NC
www.warrenpublishing.net
Printed in the United States

For Jonah and Zac, my breath and soul;
the other JH, my Batman;
and Mark, my "wasband;"
thank you for loving me, supporting me,
and never letting me quit.
I will love you always, and all ways.

xo, j

Preface

"If I just *would have* done things differently."
Woulda.
"If I *could* turn back the clock
and not be so damn impulsive."
Coulda.
"I *should have* tried harder
and not given up."
Shoulda.

Woulda. Coulda. Shoulda.
That, my friends, is the story of my life ...

And it also happens to make a perfect title for a book! Well, at least it seemed perfect when I was in the shower, washing my hair, and thought of it. Yes, for real. That's how it all started; this crazy idea for a book about how *not* to get divorced.

I'm a relationship expert, a best-selling author, and a "happily" divorced mom of two healthy, well-adjusted teenaged boys, so I bet you're all wondering why the hell I'm doing this. Why would *I* write a guide on how to *stay* married, second-guessing my own choices, and expressing so much regret?

Well, it's simple.

I fucked up! And now it's my job to stop you from doing the same.

Stay married, married people! Because divorce sucks. Plain and simple.

Oh, whatever! Are you surprised? Pick your mouth up off the floor. Even though I'm happy where I am in my life, it's all relative, okay? "Happy" and divorced looks much different than you may think it does; it pales in comparison to "unhappy" and married. In fact, being "happily divorced" may even be worse than being "miserably married."

If you are already divorced, this book is probably not for you. However, I did write *One Happy Divorce: Hold the Bulls#!t*, about making the best of a (frankly) shitty situation. (Yes, divorce can be happy, but no, it isn't ideal.) That might be helpful, or, if nothing else, I guarantee it will give you a few chuckles.

This book, *Woulda. Coulda. Shoulda.,* is for those of you contemplating a separation, or who are already in the process or talking about a divorce. If you're in couples' therapy and discussing ending your marriage, READ THIS. Maybe you're "falling out of love" at the seven-year mark? Or you just can't seem to get along after all this time. Or maybe the passion is gone? Your heart doesn't flutter when he walks in the door at the end of the day. Keep reading. I was there. I was resentful and angry because my husband didn't help with the kids as much as he should have, and, in return, he was bitter and annoyed that I expected him to after he'd worked so hard each day.

Sound familiar? Okay. This is the book for you!

If you have ever thought or talked
about, or if you are actively in the
process of getting a divorce ...

STOP.

Now, listen.

I have been divorced now for over four and a half years, and I have one of the best divorces around. My ex and I are great friends. We co-parent like champs, we are flexible, accessible, and kind to one another. Our kids are thriving and happy. Our friends ask us why we don't just get back together. (We never will, ever.) As far as divorces go, ours is as good as it gets ... and still, it is miserable. If I'd known then all the shit I know right now, I would never have done it. So, I'm here to help you—or save you, kinda—from making the biggest mistake of your life.

... Unless you are unsafe or in an unhealthy marriage. Please know that I am not advocating dangerous or abusive relationships. No way.

If you are in an unsafe environment, please call an attorney and get the hell out. Or, if need be, call the authorities and get the help you need to get to a safe place. Take the proper steps, get your finances in line, and move on. No good will come of staying in an abusive or unhealthy marriage. And your kids will never be okay if you stay where you are and continue to be mistreated. I will never advocate staying in a toxic, damaging or harmful situation. Be smart, be bold, take courage, and leave. There is help for you.

If your partner is abusive or a narcissist, run. Do not walk. This book is not for you.

Now, I understand that sometimes divorce is out of your control. For those of you whose partner came home one day and said, "I don't love you anymore," or "I'm in love with someone else," I am truly sorry ... but also somewhat relieved. You, my sweet friend, are actually lucky you got out when you did. You don't want to be where you're not wanted or loved— you deserve far better! And you will find it. If this is you, then this book is not for you, but I do encourage you to pick up a copy of *One Happy Divorce: Hold the Bulls#!t*.

I am writing this for those of you who are struggling in your relationship, or who may tend to jump without thinking. Perhaps you're impulsive, or quick to give up. You think life will be better; the grass greener.

Maybe you've heard from your divorced friends how "great" it is, right? Well, remember: misery loves company. In reality, there is nothing great about divorce. Nada. Zilch. You know those women who say, "Oh, I get so much time to myself when my ex has the kids!"? Yah, they're totally full of shit. Take it from me: being divorced is lonely and miserable. Do you really think that just because your heart doesn't "skip a beat," you should jump ship? Puh-lease. Give me a fucking break. That's just "affection" instead of "lust." It's fine to grow and change as a couple ... intimacy in a relationship has stages.

Don't throw away your best friend
for what you think is "more."

It is not more.

Again: a "miserable" marriage is far better than any "happy" divorce. I know, you think I'm crazy. I've lost my mind over here. But after reading this, you will agree! Trust me. And if you don't agree and you think you can find new love (or maybe you already have), and start a new family, good for you. Perhaps you've already "blended" with ease and there's zero animosity. Your kids are never sad; you feel no guilt. Good for you.

And I call bullshit.

Big. Piles. Of. Bullshit.

Look, I am currently in a great relationship with a fantastic man. Is it easy? No. Will it ever be? No. He has kids, I have kids. He has an ex; I have an ex. Nothing is perfect after a divorce … nothing. It's like mushing two countries together and expecting them to get along peacefully. Oh, and one country is Japan, the other is China. Or how about Israel and Iraq? Whatever, you get the point, right? It's like a warzone. No one speaks the same language or even has the same rules. But let's talk about blending later. What a shitshow!

Keep reading, friends. I was there, and I am telling you to slow your roll. Don't think for one second you're feeling (or not feeling) anything anybody else hasn't after ten years of marriage. Or twenty. I wish I'd had a divorced woman to tell me all this when I was separated, instead of a therapist nodding her head while my ex-husband and I talked. I mean, she just sat there nodding and agreeing. To tell you the truth, it just made us fight more; therapy always made us fight so much more. It brought out the worst in us, I swear. (Although, for lots of my friends, therapy was worth its weight in gold. And I do think it's always worth a shot; especially if you have children.)

Marriage can be fucking hard, but that's life, y'all.

These hard parts are what happens after being with the same partner for an extended period of time. Intimacy changes ... growth occurs, and you love differently.

Want to know a secret?

You and your partner probably loved differently to begin with. Men and women love differently. Men are all action, but women? We use our words.

What? Is this all too much for you to handle? Look, I don't have time to waste. I have marriages to save and only have a small space in which to save them. (I'm not a fan of lengthy self-help books' fluff and excess garbage.) So, I'm going to cut to the chase, hold the bullshit, and give you the goods to be successful in your journey. And how do I know what works, you ask? Because I have either lived it, or fucked it up (or both), and now I'm left with little "success-nuggets" that actually work.

So, let's get started, shall we?

Let me explain how this will all play out:

WCS is split into two parts. Part One contains all the things I wish I'd done differently in my marriage. The little "thought nuggets" are the most important tips to utilize in your everyday married life. These are all things I wish I'd gone about in a different way (for example, being kinder or sweeter), or "tactics" that I could have used instead of the approach I chose (maybe changed my tone of voice, etc.). In other words, this is all the shit I fucked up and wish I'd done right. Ha! And how much do I wish I'd had this book when I was married? If this book had been around, OMG! I would have read it over and over. Y'all are so lucky. I've done the research; worked out the kinks.

Woulda. Coulda. Shoulda.

Part Two discusses the specific things I wish I'd known about divorce before we went ahead and pulled the plug. For example: what I was about to give up and what would change. I mean, it all seems so obvious, right? You lose your house, your money, your partner .... Yah, I wish that were the extent of it, but it's not. I'm going to go deeper and delve into the harsh reality of what divorce does to your entire person. Including your social life, financial future, and health. The loss is so great it mirrors death. The only difference is the guilt that comes with divorce, knowing you may have actually been the cause of (at least parts of) the divorce.

…And you can lose the most important thing: your children. For half of their lives.

Holy fuck, right? But don't be scared! I know it sounds horrifying and depressing … and it is, to an extent. But I got ya! I mean, if you need me, that is … and I'm hoping after reading this book, you won't. Still, if divorce is inevitable, it will help to be prepared and educated; that way it will be easier (and less crappy) to manage. You can heal faster if you are informed and understand what steps need to be taken. The key word here is "if."

I was neither prepared nor educated when I got divorced. I was shocked, uninformed, and lost.

But that's why I'm doing this and sharing my opinions, experience, and research. That way you can make an informed decision to (hopefully) stay married—or be ready for what comes next if you simply cannot make it work. I hope my own mistakes will save a few marriages along the way.

And, for the record, I do not want to get remarried to my ex, nor do I wish I never got divorced. I made the right choices for my family at the time. And there is no going back. So no, I wouldn't change a thing about the direction my life has taken. My boys are settled and happy. And I'm sure some of you think I'm an ass for implying that staying in an "unhappy" marriage is better than getting a divorce.

Please keep reading.

I promise that's not what this book is about.

Every married person contemplates leaving their spouse at one time or another. If you haven't, you are not human. A happy, healthy marriage takes work and effort. It's not easy by any means; I get it. Stressors like jobs, children, money, lack of intimacy, etc. only add more problems. Maybe you've found yourself thinking about cheating or having an "emotional affair" with an old boyfriend on Facebook. Or, maybe you've found yourself wanting attention from a man who actually "uses his words." I don't think there is a single person who doesn't feel torn from time to time, wondering if something, anything would be better than what they're lying next to each night.

We are all human.

And I get it. I'm just saying, if I'd had a book like this one back when I was feeling all those feelings, I would have read it cover to cover ... twice ... then again.

And I never would have given up on my marriage.

But here we are.

Woulda. Coulda. Shoulda. ;)

PART ONE:

What I "Shoulda" Done Differently.

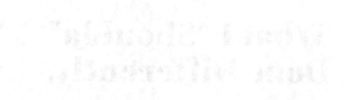

A Trip Around the Sun

Me: You're kinda hot.
Him: So are you.
Me: Wanna get married?
Him: Yeah!

And, scene!

Ummmm ... this was just about how fast the whole courtship happened for me and my wasband. I kid ... kinda. We met in Israel on a singles' mission organized by the Jewish Federation for all the leftover (loser) single people ages twenty-five to forty. We were both from Detroit, but had to fly halfway around the world to find each other. He was the most eligible bachelor; I was the town slut. Again, I kid. Kinda. Let's just say I had dated the entire city and was the last one standing. All my friends were married, and I had been exiled by my parents and told to "come back with a man." Kidding. (Okay, not kidding this time.)

The pressure was intense back in the '90s for Jewish girls to get married and pop out babies before thirty ... I was twenty-eight. My clock was ticking. And yes, my mom and dad wanted me to get hitched to a great guy and have kids, but I also wanted kids—more than anything in the world.

Since the day I could remember, I had always wanted babies. I even named them with my very first boyfriend, at summer camp. (He is reading this and dying, I'm sure.) But we did, we totally named our kids. Funniest thing? That old boyfriend ended up with three girls, not one named our girl name. And me, two boys … neither with our boy name. Ha. I guess that would be pretty fucking weird if we did use the names we chose, right?

Rhetorical.

I digress, but there wasn't a day in my life
I didn't think about having kids.

So, when I first saw Mark, my wasband, across the plane (he was the leader of the group from Detroit) I only saw "perfect sperm." (It was much like *The Perfect Storm* … only with more semen and less seamen! Ha.) No, really. It was as though his body was in the shape of an actual sperm. Like his head was a sperm head with a black Jew-fro, and his body a wiggly, lanky, spermy tail. Picture this: a giant fucking Jew-sperm walking down the aisle of a plane wearing a Tigers hat and carrying a clipboard. And now he's yelling at me to get in my seat and stop bitching. Anyway, you get my point, I saw this guy and knew he would be the most PERFECT BABY DADDY … EVER. My uterus was throbbing; all girly parts at DEFCON 1. My pistol was cocked—I had to have this man! I knew he was the guy for me, now I just had to get his attention.

For the next ten days, it became my sole mission to do anything and everything to get this man to notice me. I even went as far as falling down a flight of limestone stairs and breaking my arm. Still, he wanted nothing to do with me. How was that possible? I was hot and skinny, and I hardly complained at all. I mean, so what if I threw a fit when I didn't get an aisle seat on the plane ... and complained incessantly about the heat? Jewish girls don't do very well in the humidity. Oy!

So, I stalked him from afar. He was everything any woman could want and more. I called my little sister when I broke my arm, and she said, "Do you think you're going to land that guy with a cast up to your shoulder? Get that fucking thing off!" She was so right. It had to be the cast. I immediately chiseled the plaster cast off with a fork. Still, nada.

As the days passed, I was more certain than ever he was everything I was searching for. He was successful, driven, brilliant ... and Jewish, of course. The Perfect Sperm. I was on the hunt, and nothing was going to stop me, even though nothing seemed to work. That only made me want him more.

But it wasn't until the last night of the trip that he even talked to me. I asked him if he wanted to take a picture for my scrapbook. He said, "Umm, what was your name, again?" OMG. I was in love, and he had just spoken to me. (Okay, so he didn't even know who I was ... whatever.) He was perfection. I laughed as I flipped my hair, and asked if when we got home, he'd "maybe want to go for coffee?" He said, "I don't drink coffee. How about a beer?" Yes! A beer. I'd have to start drinking beer. I'd make that happen. Whatever it took.

It was three weeks later when we finally went on our first date, since I was totally playing hard to get. (Okay, I was actually sitting by my answering machine making sure the batteries were still working, wondering why he wasn't calling. Crying. Whining. Waiting. Ahem.) When we finally went out, I looked at him and said, "You know what? I'm totally going to marry you." He looked back at me, white as a ghost, and said, "You are fucking crazy, Jennifer."

Be still my beating heart!

Ten months later we were engaged. Eight months after that, married. And six months after that, we had our first kid.

So, what's my point?

And why the long-ass story?

Stay with me ….

I know. Most of you reading this are already married. You're probably thinking, "How does this information help me?" or "Why do we care?" I want you to hear this story, because it was such an "ah-ha" moment in my divorce. It's when I realized, "OMG, maybe getting hitched too soon or not spending enough quality time with my hubby prior to having kids was most likely a factor in our bickering early on in our marriage." Yasss! Do you agree? Are you sitting there nodding and thinking, maybe if I woulda waited a little longer, traveled a bit, or spent more quality time getting to know my husband, we wouldn't have even gotten married in the first place? Bingo!

Woulda. Coulda. Shoulda.

This is where I wish Mark and I had done what my good friend, Rhoberta Shaler, likes to call "a trip around the sun." Yes! "Trip around the sun" is an idea I'd never heard of until recently when I had this fantastic guest, Rhoberta Shaler, PhD, on my podcast, Doing Divorce Right. She's a relationship expert and she said, "You have to date a man for at least a 'trip around the sun' before you marry him." Yes! A trip around the sun! How dang cute is that? We all need to slow the hell down. One full year, or no ring. Want to know why? Well, duh! You don't know a person until you've spent time with them. You can't see their true colors until you have dated them through all four seasons.

I actually tell my clients they have a ninety-day rule. I won't let them even call it a real "relationship" until they have been dating for three full months!

And not every relationship is going to end in marriage. (In fact, not every person wants to get married.) Some relationships are to teach you what you don't want in a partner, and others may teach you about yourself. Not every man has to be "the one." And guys, not every woman wants to have babies (or at least with you). Point being, don't go into every relationship with marriage as the end game. Try going on dates with a positive attitude and a smile. Men love a woman who exudes confidence and a zest for life. (Not a woman dying to get hitched.) Dating should be a marathon, not a sprint. One of the biggest mistakes women make is to not take their time and really learn about the man sitting next to them.

Make sure it's more than just a physical attraction too. Attraction will fade, and you must love what is left behind ... a good friendship.

How can you know who a person really, truly is if you haven't spent time learning and growing together? Everyone is on their best behavior at the start of a relationship. And when you are in the beginning stages of intimacy, the "lust stage," everything feels good and right. You're wearing "rose-colored glasses," and her faults are not really faults at all. Or his bad-habits may not seem "that bad." You are so filled with the love hormone Oxytocin, you can actually miss certain negative things that you might see further down the road. Your brain is undergoing both chemical and hormonal changes. You're in the "honeymoon period," baby! No real-life, long-term decisions should be made during this time, especially whether you actually want to get married. The answer will always be a resounding, "YES!"

So, wait. Be patient, people.

A year is my new rule: a trip around the sun!

If I would have (woulda) spent a bit more time getting to know Mark before we got engaged, maybe we could have (coulda) seen that we were not as compatible as we thought we were. Or perhaps we could have prevented some of the "issues" we had early on in our relationship. Now, of course, hindsight is twenty-twenty.

And for the record, I wouldn't have changed a single thing about my marriage, because then I wouldn't have my Jonah and Zac. But I'm hoping someone who is reading this and still dating or thinking about getting engaged will learn to *sloooow* it down and enjoy one another.

Be sure to breathe and take time to be together before you rush so fast into a family. Does that make sense? Wait for the honeymoon phase to be over so you can wake up and smell the roses! You might actually find yourself in a bit of shock, facing some not-so-comfortable truths about the person you thought you knew so well. The honeymoon phase can last between six and eighteen months in some cases, so spend your time really getting to know your mate before you pop the question. … And even longer before you make the leap into parenthood.

Now go on, get out of here until it's been at least twelve months, you little love bird.

... Did you wait? Good. Okay, now does your partner have any nasty habits you can't stand in the long term? How about political views that may throw a wrench in your plans? Does it utterly disgust you that she chews with her mouth open, or he never changes his sheets on the bed? And more importantly, can you live with these things? When the "in-love" phase ends, and the rose-colored glasses come off ... can you still love the person standing in front of you and live the rest of your life with him or her? If the answer is "yes," then good. It's time to replace that infatuation with respect and affection ... and genuinely learn to love this person.

Time, my friends ... and a trip around the sun.

*And thank you, Dr. Rhoberta Shaler, PhD. for sharing that tasty little thought-nugget with me!

Don't Forget About Us

Me: Do you have kids?
Friend: Nope. We don't want them.
Me: Oh. Can I ask why?
Friend: ... We want to stay married.

Ask a married couple without kids how they are doing, and the answer is always, "Fantastic!" or, "We're great!" or, "What is there to be unhappy about?" Yah. Well, fuck you too, kidless people.

Of course, you're smiling.

You don't have kids!

Oh, shut up. You know I'm only saying exactly what you're thinking. You wish you had the balls to say it, but you don't: *kids ruin marriages.* Yup, and it's not even their fault. They were just born to do it! And the worst thing? We asked them to. We wanted them to ... in fact, we even chose to have them at specific times in our lives. Some of us wanted them so badly we made them in test tubes or petri dishes, or took tons of drugs or injections, or adopted them! Fuck, I wanted mine so badly I played with my vaginal fluid, took my temperature, and then put my legs over my head after we had sex.

Plain and simple, we all wanted our kids.

… Even though they inherently ruined our lives.

And I'm not even kidding. Kids do. But we love them anyway, right? (Rhetorical.) Now let's go back to our pre-parenthood lives just for shits and giggles. Back before you had your kids, it was just you and your hubby (or wife). You could do anything you wanted to do, whenever you wanted to do it. You slept in every morning, stayed up and had sex, or watched television. You made noise, talked on the phone, ate sugar cereal. Shit, you even traveled to places that didn't have big talking mice or baby pools. And didn't you love a table for just two? *Ahhhh,* the good old days. You *both* went to work and had adult conversations about life or television shows you watched (without purple dinosaurs). Exercising on the weekends was done sans a stroller or some contraption glued to your person. And money was never an issue. Money. What the hell is money? Ohhhh … money! It's green and grown on trees! Yes. It was just the two of you. "Us" and "we." *Awww!*

And then your kids were born. Yay.

We still love those little fuckers! Wouldn't change it for the world. But let's just be honest for the purpose of this book. Shit started to get pretty dang stressful when that first kid was born, am I right? All of a sudden, your table of two became three, and you were automatically responsible for another living being besides yourself. *Ummm, is there some kind of manual that comes with this pint-sized human, 'cause I'm not so sure I get this?*

It started off pretty cool, right? The new stuff, bottles, and diapers. You paint the room and buy all the baby gear. A shower for the new momma, then it's a sprinkle for the second kid. That, my friends, is new. I never had a sprinkle! Hell, Jews don't even get baby showers! And what the flip is this new thing with "gender reveal" parties? Oh, hell! Whose idea was it to kick a dang football or launch a fucking rocket to find out if your kid has a penis? What happened to just looking for those three little lines on the ultrasound screen that are supposedly your kid's vagina? Awww, look at the tiny little vajay-jay! (Like you could really tell if that blur was a penis ....)

But then it happens.

The baby is born.

And he becomes the most crucial thing in the world.

To everyone.

I once had a friend tell me she loved her husband more than her children. I shit you not. She totally did; not even kidding. I hated her after that. I never quite looked at her the same. She actually said that her kids were "replaceable," but her husband was not, and while she could always have another child with her husband, she could never get another "him." I lost all respect for her as a person; a mother. Our friendship was never truly the same. Can you imagine that? As a mother, saying out loud that you would let someone shoot your child before he shot your husband? Maybe I'm being a bit judgy, but hell!

See, the minute my kids came out of my body ... they instantly became first. Numero uno. And that's what I believe *should* happen. You should put your kids first, and moms just do. And dads? Well, they have to learn how to do it … kinda.

But they never really do. I mean, do they?

Honestly?

See, moms will always put the kids first, because that's what moms do. That's what I did, and I would not have changed it. It will never be part of my Woulda. Coulda. Shoulda.

I have told Mark over and over I had to put the boys first and him second. Jonah needed me; he has Asperger's Syndrome. Well, *had* Asperger's Syndrome. We like to say he "fell off the spectrum;" basically he's "cured." Jonah had so much therapy before the age of three, you'd never even notice anything different if you met him now. We are beyond blessed. He was diagnosed at twenty-two months old and early intervention became my full-time job. So, I digress, but being there for my kids was just what I had to do as a mom.

But here is the catch … listening? Dads put work first because it is in their beings to take care of their families. And the only way to support the family is *how*? To work and make the money, right? So, when those of us who are exhausted, stay-at-home moms bitch and moan at our working husbands … what happens to our marriages? It puts stress on our relationship and resentment begins to build. Mom gets angry that Dad isn't pulling his weight at home with the house and kids; Dad isn't feeling appreciated for the hard, tireless work he's doing to support the family … and BOOM!

There we have it.

And what about working mommas? In many cases, it seems you all are still responsible for your kiddos and the house on top of your full-time jobs! What in the actual fuck is that? So many of my friends who are full-time working moms do more for the kids than the dads do; it's just in our nature, gals. Is it fair? Not really. But is it life? Yup. Most of the time!

And so, the story goes … everyone is stressed, resentful, and exhausted.

All this mishegas (oh, that's craziness in Yiddish) is from having kids. Everyone acts like it's the kids' fault, and the poor kids don't even know it. I mean, how can they possibly be to blame for something they had absolutely zero part of?

Now that we know the heart of the issue, let's fix it.

Here is where I wish I'd done things better.

I coulda done more to help Mark feel appreciated; and I shoulda helped my family.

That's it! Don't forget about the "us."

Go back to the pre-parenthood part of this and read it again. Think back to when the kids were not part of the family dynamic and find the "us" again. I remember how angry I was at Mark for leaving me all day with the boys. I was covered in Zac-puke and Jonah was in therapy all day. I'm crying as I think about how I never greeted him at the door with a smile on my face; a hug or a kiss. I was so resentful and mad. If I only had thought about the "us." I *shoulda* just stopped and said, "I appreciate all you're doing for us, Mark;" or, "Let's just *us* go out to dinner tonight. I'll get my mom to watch the boys;" or, "How about *just us* go to a movie?" That doesn't sound hard, right? Pause. Consider all that your husband or wife does each day. Appreciate them. And find the *us* again.

I forgot about us.

The kids came first for me, and that was okay. Work came first for Mark, and that was what paid our bills and Jonah's therapy … so that was okay too. But somewhere in between, we forgot about *us* in all the messy shit (sometimes literally) of being a parent. Finding a date night once a week, or meeting in the bathroom for kissing time. Putting the kids in front of a movie and having a glass of wine and a conversation in which you are not allowed to mention the kids. Making time for each other and for fuck's sake! Be thankful for what each of you brings to the table.

And listen, because this part's important. Whether you're a SAHM or you work out of the house, he should appreciate what you do as well. Own your shit! It's okay if he works hard to support the family, and you work hard to take care of the kids. (Or you work at a job that pays more than his and he stays at home and plays Mr. Mom.) Whatever your situation, appreciate and respect one another.

Keep in mind that one day when they are gone and in college, the Family Pyramid will flip again and the two will be alone. Suddenly it will be back to just the two of you, and then you can congratulate each other on how awesome of a job you did, or how you can't believe you survived it all. The late nights, teaching them how to drive, their first dates, and last homecoming game. Watching them become young adults and hoping they come home safely every time they leave the house. Loving them so much, you can't imagine a day without them under your roof. (Oh, and just remember, it is entirely the kids' fault for everything … but they won't know it until they are parents.)

Let's keep it our little secret. ;)

The Balls are in HIS Court

Me: I got it.
Him: I can do it.
Me: But can you do it MY way?

"I mean, if you are going to move that slowly, just let me do it myself!" I say, pushing him out of the way and taking one of his testicles as I exit.

Yeesh. Was I really that bad? Ummm, yes. I was really that bad. No, actually, I was worse. And if we are being honest, so were most of my friends. I don't think any of my friends' husbands got their balls back until their kids were in their teens. What a nightmare! The way I hear my friends speak to their poor husbands is embarrassing and pathetic. I feel sick to my stomach and apologize to Mark every time I see him for the way I used to treat him when we were married.

Every. Single. Time.

Part of me thinks it was hormonal. I was a hot mess after Jonah was born. I almost killed my father-in-law at Rosh Hashanah dinner for waking Jonah after I had finally got him to sleep after seven hours of trying. I mean, really? The poor man just wanted to give his grandson a squeeze and I all but attacked him. So, for real, hormones played a huge part in my bitchiness post-partum with my kiddos.

… But I had no excuse when they were nine. (Oops.) I just thought I could do everything better and faster than my husband. Yup! I was the mom, so my way was more efficient. And for real, why did it take him so fucking long to change diapers? Come on, Hot Stuff, we got places to be! It made me crazy.

But do I feel sorry for being such an enormous crotch?

Yes, I do.

If I could do shit differently, I would have been nicer to Mark. I would have been more appreciative of him, thanked him for all he provided for our family. I was always so angry because he "got to go to work" and have adult conversations while I was stuck at home with the boys. *Stuck?* Okay, I loved it. I was "happily stuck"—and I wanted that! It's what I had asked for, and I wouldn't have it any other way.

Despite the fact that I had wanted to be a stay-at-home mom, the minute Mark walked in the door each night, I wanted so badly to throw the kids at him. I was so pissed, I sometimes acted like he didn't deserve to be there. Can you even believe that? I would be giving Jonah a bath and Mark would walk in the room and I'd say, "Oh, look who decided to show up tonight, Jonah. It's your daddy." Jesus! I was horrible. Horribly resentful, horribly angry, just plain fucking horrible. I was passive aggressive and would do things like refold clothes he folded because it wasn't done exactly the way I wanted it done.

Fuck, y'all! I would've done so many things differently. I would have done them with a smile and said "thank you." I *shoulda* made the choice to be happy. It is a conscious choice, after all. And my anxiety caused so much strife in our house. I had so many insecurities about my parenting and being a good mother. Mark told me all the time that the boys would be okay, but I didn't believe him. Like how did *he* know? He was just the dad! I needed to see for myself, *do* everything for myself. … *And* I made Mark feel inadequate, which only made matters worse. Jonah was more stressed (kids with Asperger's, actually all kids, pick up on the stress around them), and Mark was upset because he thought he sucked. In the long run, what did my need to control the universe solve? Zilch. And ya know what else? Because I always thought *my* way was the only way, I ended up doing everything!

What the hell?

I had the hardest time relinquishing control.

Aha! There it is. The real issue is the *control factor.* So many women find it nearly impossible to just let other people help them. These women treat others as if they are incapable or less than. Some don't even realize they're doing it. Hmmm … honestly, I am not sure I even knew I let my controlling get so out of, well, control! But here is the truth:

Men LOVE to help!

Men are born helpers and fixers.

And they want to save us and protect us. So, ask for help, girls.

Ask, and you shall receive. Watch how much easier your life becomes when you admit other people can do things just as well as you. And remember this: it's ok that the "help" you're getting isn't perfectly perfect, either. So-the-fuck-what if the wine glasses are on the bottom rack of the dishwasher?

And who really cares if your kid's socks match? Hey, at least he's wearing them! Kudos to your hubby! And congrats to you for relinquishing control.

I know, that whole relinquishing control thing was super hard for me. It took years of work. And even medication. Hey, I'm not embarrassed one bit to admit it. I believe in taking care of your mental health first and foremost. Shit, if I hadn't been on meds for my anxiety, I'm not sure how I would've handled taking care of two kids under the age of two (one with special needs). And I do believe even coaches need coaches; therapy is good for the soul. (All souls, male or female.)

So, do me a favor: ask your man to help you make the kids' lunches or build a new desk … see how fast he comes running. But there's one catch: ask, then walk away. Yes, I'm serious. Let him do it *his* way and tell him how damn good it looks or how much you appreciate the job well done. Use your words and see his reaction.

See how quickly he surprises you by doing something else without you even asking.

Just the other day, I was missing my man. Oh! I have a fantastic guy in my life now. Well, it's been almost two years, but who's counting? (ME!) We met online three years ago, went on a date that sucked shit, and parted ways. But, we stayed really good friends! Then, after a year as friends, we found each other again and decided to give it another go. There is so much more to this story, but who has the time? So, we got back together, and it's been me and the Batman for the past twenty-three months. Ha, Batman. It's his nickname on my social media, but his real name is Jim. Don't ask, just go check us out. He's my funny guy. I truly adore him; he's my rock.

So, I digress ... The other day I was missing Jim, and feeling a bit "disconnected." I called him and asked him to please come over because I "needed him" to record a podcast episode with me. He said, "Really, babe? Okay, well then. If you need me, I'm on my way." No questions asked. If I had asked him any other way it might not have played out so perfectly. For example, if I had said, "Honey, can you come over later and record a show?" or "I know you're probably tired, but can you come over?" He might have said "no." It's the secret word that got him. *I need you, honey.* Try it next time, and be sweet. Use it with almost anything you want him to do for you. But appreciate the effort and love his work.

... And let him keep his balls.

No man likes to be emasculated (duh). Still, I was the best at making my ex-husband feel like shit. And I am not proud of my behavior. Did I mean to be so awful? I don't think I did. I was miserable and exhausted; overwhelmed and hormonal. No excuse, but it is what it is. And it wasn't until right after my divorce was final four years ago that I had an "ah-ha" moment that slapped me in the face.

I was at a weekend retreat for women called "Campowerment," in the mountains of Malibu, California. This "sleepaway camp-inspired" experience is just for women ... and it's perfectly designed to help reignite your life. OMG, this is my happy place. So, I was sitting in a workshop with one of my favorite life coaches, Andrea Quinn, and she was teaching about the importance of relinquishing control and allowing yourself to receive help. As I listened, I became overwhelmed with emotion, and had to excuse myself from the group. I found a cell signal and called Mark. Without letting him even say hello, I began apologizing for the way I had treated him during our marriage. It was funny, he said he didn't think I was "that bad" and to "stop beating myself up."

But when you are sitting alone on a mountain, overlooking the Pacific Ocean off the coast of Malibu, and thinking about your failed marriage and how you've just left your kids without the family they deserved ...

It is tough not to beat yourself up.

Marriage is hard work, but divorce is harder. Hell, all relationships are difficult. And although I wouldn't get back together with Mark—we are in such a solid place and the boys are well-adjusted and thriving—I would have loved to do things right by him. And I know Mark feels the same way; if not for me, at least for our boys.

Woulda. Coulda. Shoulda. ;)

TOUCHY FEELY

Me: Ugh. Not. Now.
Him: Really? It's been six weeks.
Me: Let's make it seven.

Y
ou wake up at the crack of ass, roll out of bed, and walk down the hall to the nursery. You pick the baby up out of the crib and put him on your boob. You still smell of puke from the night before, and you didn't even have time to brush your teeth. The little fella was crying when you walked into his room, but he smelled so sweet when you picked him up. He is your life. Your soul. Your breath. Nothing else in the world matters now as you rock him; you fall asleep with him in your arms.

Nothing else matters.

You look up as your husband walks into the nursery to say goodbye for work, but you don't really care. He kisses the baby and then the top of your head. *Ugh, does he have to kiss you?* You hardly respond. He mutters something about being late because of a meeting with the boss ... but you are too busy switching breasts and burping the baby to reply.

You are busy.
He is busy.

You hardly see each other anymore, like two ships … does it really matter? I mean, you'll "find each other again" when the kids are older, right? So what if you haven't had sex in six weeks? Some of your friends haven't had sex in six months! We are normal; this is the norm, right? No one has an active sex life when they have small children; they are too tired and crabby … right?

I don't even want to touch him, he makes my skin crawl. He thinks I'm fat, I'm sure. I mean, I *am* still pretty chubby. And he says he's exhausted from work anyway. It's fine! We will make up for it next month on our vacation to Miami. I'm not worried …

Here's a secret:

Worry.

Worry a lot.

In fact, if you're not having sex at least once a week, things are not where they should be, and I'm about to get REAL up in here. Are you ready? Batten down the hatches and get busy. If you haven't blown that horn recently, you ships passing in the night better drop your anchors, mount the crow's nest, and make some waves, because this relationship expert is calling *BULLSHIT!*

According to the Kinsey Institute, a "sexless marriage" is one in which a committed couple has sex fewer than ten times per year. Now, about fifteen to twenty percent of long-term couples actually fall into this category. (I know, right?) Currently, studies done by Princeton University show that infrequent sex is an issue. In fact, they show that lack of sex corresponds directly with marital instability and thoughts of leaving a relationship.

Well, duh! I mean, if you're not fucking your spouse, he is going to find someone who will. (Preach!) And trust me, fellas, if you're not giving your wife the emotional (and physical) attention she needs, she'll be online getting told how hot she is by her college boyfriend. And I wish I were kidding. This is one of the most prevalent issues with social media to date.

> "57% of men and 54% of women who have cheated in one relationship will cheat in future relationships, especially with the ease of emotional infidelity access on Facebook."
>
> –BRANDONGAILLE.COM

Oh, did I mention I don't sugar coat this shit? Yah. Well, there it is. Sex and intimacy are the most important parts of a marriage. Did you get that? Wait, I'll say it again ... SEX IS THE SECRET SAUCE to a successful marriage. Dammit. I just gave away the whole farm. As if you didn't know? But herein lies the disconnect: Oftentimes, one partner's sex drive doesn't match the other's. Maybe one person wants it more frequently, which poses a problem. But hang on, people, I got ya. There are reasons behind this and you just need to be open for discussion and willing to talk about the why:

- Why do you want to have sex five days a week and your husband would be fine having it once a month?
- Why does he only want to have sex on the weekends and you are into morning sex?
- Why do you think he used to be more attracted to you and now, not so much?
- Why are you feeling more tired than usual?

Let's figure this out here and now, together. Get talking and if you need to get a sex coach or therapist, do it! I know some of the best on hand; reach out and we can set you up. There is nothing to be ashamed of or embarrassed about. Your marriage is at stake, y'all! It's so important to be able and willing to have the tough conversations, because the longevity and success of your marriage depends on it. You can do it! And I think you will find, the minute you start talking, your partner will too. It just takes one person to open the door to communication and the other to be willing to walk through it. Help each other. It is not always a comfortable or easy conversation to have. Not everyone is as open about sex, or sexual dysfunction, and many men feel threatened when approached. So, make it light and fun!

LET'S TALK ABOUT SEX ... UAL INHIBITIONS.

Here is a list of things that could be causing a dip in libido for both sides. If any of these sound familiar, tell your partner and discuss:
- Age
- Life circumstances
- Physical health
- Emotional health
- Kids in house
- Pregnancy/hormones
- Certain medications
- Hormonal imbalance
- Loss or grief
- Substance abuse
- Workload or stress
- Relationship status (separated/divorced)
- Intimacy issues
- Trust, secrets, or relationship issues

LET'S GET BUSY!

(Tips for how to get more of what you want ... SEX!)

SCHEDULE IT!

Okay, now I know this sounds nuts, and horrifically unromantic ... but quite the contrary! Scheduling your sex is smart, and it actually works. And, it's super-sexy! I have a girlfriend who's been married for over twenty years, and she's the one who turned me on to this little trick. I shit you not! Every week she and her hubby have sex on Friday nights (and only on Friday night). They both know it's coming (pun intended) and they get excited, prepared, and all hot for the date. She shaves and picks out a sexy nightie; he is turned on all day thinking about getting laid that evening. And do you know what one of the number one aphrodisiacs is? You guessed it—anticipation! So, she might even send him a hot text during the day reminding him of their "sex date," or he sometimes leaves a little sticky note on the bedroom mirror. I love it!

And on the flip side, there is no pressure to have sex on any other day of the week. So they can both relax and just enjoy each other's company; sans that "the elephant in the room." Ya know? Wondering if he wants to have sex tonight, but you're so dang tired. You don't want to ... but you're worried he will feel rejected. So, you do it anyway, not really feeling it. He knows you don't really want it, and feels bad, "like he's twisting your arm." Then you both end up feeling shitty and unwanted.

There is nothing worse than a man feeling rejected,
or a woman feeling unwanted.

Ugh! I can remember lying next to Mark after being pissed and shit on all day by the babies and thinking, "Please, G–d. Don't touch me." I would lay really, really still and hope he would fall asleep. I know, so pathetic, but I didn't want to hurt his feelings. I never wanted to reject him outright. And other times, I would want him so fucking bad! I'd get all up in his shit, or start to go down on him. Pushing me off of him he'd say, "Honey, I'm so tired, just not feeling it." OMG! I thought I would die, feeling totally unwanted and rejected by my own husband. I'd end up using my vibrator in the bathroom and going to bed.

Fuck, the worst.

If only I knew then what I know now, y'all. I would have scheduled a sex night! I would have had hot, romantic, amazing sex with my husband and rocked his world. Because you know even when you don't really want to have it, after you start going—and get all hot and turned on—it's the best. And when you have that killer orgasm, don't you always say, "Why don't we do that more often?" Ha. I know we always did. Every single time.

I remember the two of us laughing so hard after we were done making love and saying we promised to do it more often. … But then it was weeks until the next time. … Then months. Life just got in the way of life. And our paths stopped crossing in the bedroom. I started resenting him more; he pulled away. Intimacy is so hard to find once it's lost, y'all. And once it's gone, it is almost impossible to get it back. But don't give up! You can get it back, it just takes effort on *both* parts. If I could just have done it differently, I would have loved more—loved him more, and made love more often.

So, to my friends who are still banging after twenty years of marriage (scheduled or not!), kudos to you! And for those of you who are struggling to find each other in the darkness of your bedrooms ... look harder. (Pun intended. Ha.) Keep looking, and find each other.

MIX IT UP.

Ever see that episode of "Modern Family" where Phil and Claire meet at the bar, pretend they don't know each other, and plan a secret rendezvous to get away from the kids? *Yaaaasss.* Roleplay, people! Do you have a secret fantasy you want to share and act out? Teacher/student, perhaps? Ha. Who knows ... just make it happen. Call him "Daddy!" Listen, if that's all it takes to get him hot in the bedroom ... do it, gurl! Just put on those sexy red heels and let him call you by another name. Your marriage is at stake here, ladies! ;)

GET OUT OF TOWN.

Nothing says sexy like a change of scenery and a bottle of tequila. Ole! Head to the beach, or the mountains. Shit, any hotel will do! Just get out of your house, and into a new bedroom. Bed and breakfast for one night, a city skyline as your view ... just have sex on someone else's sheets. Make a mess and let the housekeeper clean it up! If all else fails, do it in the kitchen instead of the bedroom. (I'm digging deep, peeps!)

LOVE IS IN THE AIR.

You think you're the only one who likes to be romanced? Guess again! Make a mix-tape (or playlist for you youngsters) with his favorite songs, send a flirty-text, or write a note with a lipstick kiss. Tell him you love him just because, or whisper you'll be naked when he gets home from work. Plan a surprise date that involves things he likes to do, even if you're not a fan. Make him his favorite food or wrap up a piece of lingerie and have him open it ... then model it for him.

Remember, you can be intimate without actually having sex and just holding hands is enough too. Reach across the table at dinner and touch him ... brush against his leg at dinner. I love it when my boyfriend opens my car door, then leans in to kiss me ... he does it every time. Sexy as fuck! And he holds my hand while he's driving, and I always hold his face while we kiss. Touching is so important when it comes to showing affection and love. He may not always use his words, but I know when he reaches for my hand while we are watching TV ... he loves me.

ANTICIPATION.

Wait. For. It.

Nothing is hotter than making someone want it. Whatever "it" is. Whether it's that very first kiss or prolonging an orgasm ... anticipation is an aphrodisiac in itself. So, use it to your advantage! Send a text to him at work saying you're hot for him and you can't wait until he gets home. Or ask him to meet you for a "quickie" at lunch. I promise if you make coming home at night a pleasant experience instead of a total pain in the ass, your man will be home much sooner than later. In fact, he might even suggest you meet the girls for Happy Hour after work, and he will grab the kiddos from daycare. Or better yet, maybe y'all grab a sitter and meet after work for dinner out on the town.

JUST GOT PAID.

Ok, this might sound nuts, but it works for a whole lot of my friends. Now, just hear me out. Some of us females might need a little "incentive" to get the ball rolling in the bedroom. (I'm just saying!) Now, I'm not insinuating you should ever be treated like a prostitute or anything (unless that is roleplay you enjoy!), but what if a new pair of shoes turned you on? Ha! I actually have a number of friends who get a new "item" from their hubbies each time they give a blowjob or have sex.

Come on! Whatever it takes ... DO IT! This is how important sex and intimacy are, people. And after a few times, you might think this is fun and make a game of it! Maybe you offer to clean the house for cunnilingus? Or cook his favorite meal if he tries something new he's said he would *never* do in the past. I love this idea! Damn, I'm good, right? ;)

DISSAPEARING ACT.

Here's one I learned from a coach I love, Marnie Nir, who is funnier than you even know. I worship her. She taught me this fun little game to play with your spouse. Ready? I think I'm changing it a bit, but it's ok. Pick a day to have sex each week and if you don't stick to the plan, you lose something you love. Ha. Like for me, I *love* my glass of wine, for others it might be Monday Night Football. Some might love chocolate or working out. Following me? So, if you and your partner make a pact to have sex every Friday night and one of you "breaks the deal," that person loses the thing they love! So, I would lose my glass of wine for the week. Or, Jim would lose his CrossFit workout the next day. (Oh, fuck, he would die!)

So, in other words ... you both better show up for that sex date (unless you have, I don't know, diarrhea or something ...

nobody wants that!). If your favorite Netflix show of the week is that important, trust me, you'll show up naked and fuck your hubby. ;)

BAG OF TRICKS.

Ok, this is an oldie but goodie, but I've made it a little hipper! Grab a mason jar or cute bag and cut up some blank pieces of paper. Grab your man, and head for the bedroom … fully clothed. Sit on the bed, divide the pieces of paper, and put the jar in the middle of the bed. Oh, and make sure you have pens to write with. Now, lock the door or get a babysitter, and please, brush your teeth, y'all, because shit is about to go down!

Next, each of you writes five things you want to do in bed, or fantasies, or maybe parts of your body you want touched. You make up the rules, just write some sexy shit on those little pieces of paper and shove them in the jar or bag. Do you get it? Then, each of you take turns picking one at a time out of the jar … and talk about what you pick … or better yet, just start doing it! Trust me, if you start by just reading, you will end up naked anyway.

And who doesn't love being naked with the one you love? ;)

Pitch Perfect

Me: Are you listening to me?
Him: ... What?
Me: Didn't you hear me?
Him: Yah, unfortunately.

I laughed as I wrote that little blurb above. I mean, really? Don't you wonder if they hear us at all when we are talking? What the hell! Sometimes it's like we are talking right through them; they sit there like deer in headlights. Why? I know he's got to be hearing me. I'm yelling, for the love of all things holy—the entire neighborhood hears what I'm saying! Hmmm.

Maybe that's the problem ...
he has tuned me out!

Maybe my tone has caused him to ignore everything I'm saying, and now he's using selective hearing and not understanding a word I'm saying at all.

Bingo, bitches!

And if you keep that shit up, sooner or later your guy will not only tune you out ... but he will be running for the flipping door. No guy likes being talked to in that tone of voice. (Screaming from the other room), "OMG ... honey!

How many times do I have to tell you to pick up your wet towel off the floor?" No man wants to be spoken to like he's a two-year-old child. "Jesus, did you not hear me the first time?" And that sour-ass tone will stop any man in his tracks. "Why can't we get the marble floor? Didn't you make enough money this month?" He will shut down as fast as you can say "Screaming Mimi." Check yourself and learn how to keep your tone under control when you're addressing any conflict in your relationship.

I know this was (and always will be) a massive issue for me. I'm a hot little thing! I go from zero to sixty in about two and a quarter seconds, and when I get hot, I get *hot*. My voice gets loud, I start talking fast, and sometimes I can't stop myself. Some of us are just screamers, and others are lucky enough to be calm, cool, and collected. Personality plays a prominent role in this too, but it means some of us need to work harder than others to control ourselves when we get going.

Me? I'm a Jewish girl from Detroit, yeesh!

But the first step to fixing this conversation quandary is admitting you play a part in the problem. Then, identify a strategy to utilize when you feel yourself getting heated. Some of us don't even realize we are raising our voices! (Notice how I got all loud up in here? Ha.) For example, sometimes Jim will start yelling at me and have absolutely no idea he's yelling. Then when I call him on it, he looks at me like I'm nuts. I also have a problem controlling my mouth and what comes out of it. I'm impulsive and sometimes what I say can be hurtful, even though I don't intend it to be. I can forget who I am talking to and that my partner is not the villain. When possible, I try to maintain a calm, even tone of voice so I can be heard and understood. And when I'm just venting about a problem or talking about my day, I need to remember my boyfriend is not my verbal punching bag.

It's essential to maintain your tone,
pitch, and volume when talking, venting,
or arguing; all of us need to.
People, we need to check ourselves!

Jim and I will be discussing something as silly as which team should make pro football's "big game" this year, and he's like, "Why the hell are you yelling at me?" And I am like, "I'M NOT YELLING. DO YOU WANT TO HEAR YELLING?" I also do this with my kids, and I'm fully aware it's not very nice. In fact, it's pretty condescending and rude. But I'm just so mad! I know you totally get what I'm talking about, gals, because this is actually an exact conversation I've had with a group of girlfriends. Three out of the five all agreed to having the same words with their partners. Not just similar, but they used the exact same phrase, "I'm not yelling … do you want to hear me yell?" Funny, huh?

Ahem. Maybe not.

I try to explain that my "yelling" is really just me getting "passionate" and "overly excited" about the topic at hand. But Jim thinks I'm all amped up and ready with my gloves on. He immediately goes on the defensive because he feels like he's being attacked. Can you blame him? Ugh, we are so different, men and women, right? And by the time I'm into the important part of the conversation, he is so turned-off, I have completely shut him down without even trying. It can feel almost impossible to stay cool, calm, and collected when I have to get my point across. Anyone else feel this way? Well, if you have a vag, I'm sure you're yelling right now in agreeance. Ha.

Look, when I was married, I was pleasant to the mailman. Kind to the guy at the grocery store bagging my shit. I even invited my manicurist to our wedding for fuck's sake. And I always used this high-pitched, sweet little voice when I spoke to people who were older than me, or who I didn't know. And if I ever met someone from Mark's work, my voice got even sweeter and higher. But when I spoke to Mark, it was the "real me." Sometimes even nasty; venting all the time about my shit. So not fair to him!

Mark would say, "It's so crazy, the whole world gets Nice Jen, and me and the boys get you unhappy and miserable." It was almost like I used all my "nice" on the people who didn't deserve or need it. The people I didn't or shouldn't have given one iota about. It was Mark and the boys who deserved my "nice" and "happy," not strangers. Jesus, I sound like a real prize, huh? Still, I bet there are some of you reading this and nodding along. You know what I'm talking about; what I'm describing hits so close to home. I swore I would watch how I expressed myself in my next relationship after my divorce. I am getting better, kinda. Okay, I am working on it.

Old habits are hard to break, a work in progress. I am always a work in progress.

So, tonight, when your hubby gets home from work (or he's home, and you walk in the door from your day), greet him at the door and ask him how he's doing. And instead of talking, listen. *Speak less, listen more.* Let him tell you about his day, his job. Ask open-ended questions that have answers you might have to think about to understand. Mark said I never asked him about his career. *Ummm, wow.* Well, why would I? His job was boring and for brilliant guys. He was the head of some big bank and dealt with money and numbers. I was tired, and couldn't really give a rat's ass what he did.

... I mean, as long as we had a membership to the country club. Oh, and that new Range Rover. The white one I always wanted with chrome rims. And the boys could go to the best private school in North Carolina, naturally. And the big house in the best part of town ... why did it matter *what* he did? As long as I got to do what I wanted, why was *his* life important? (Ummm, hello! I'm not really a piece of shit, just exaggerating for effect to prove my point here. You do see what I mean, right, girls? Ok, phew.)

Those of you who are sitting exactly where I was six years ago, on the verge of separation ... does it sound familiar? That's okay. 'Cause you still have time to fix it. Save your marriage and start appreciating the fuck out of the man who gives you the life you deserve.

You do deserve it. The life, I mean. And I did too. I worked hard, raised two of the most amazing boys, and I gave up my career for them and Mark. But I also got to stay home every day and watch those boys take their first steps, and say their first words. ("Mommy," of course, not "Daddy.")

And he missed it all.

Because he was working his ass off to make a perfect, beautiful life for us.

I'm not saying I was a horrible bitch and I was the only reason we divorced, okay? It takes two to tango. However, if I'd known all of this (and I did, but couldn't admit it) and I'd had the chance to *fix* it, I would have! Or at least I would have tried a little harder ....

It's as simple as Do, Re, Me ... just by changing your tone. ;)

Enough is Enough

Me: Did you take out the trash?
Him: Not yet.
Me: Good thing I did it already.

Well, if you already took out the trash, why the hell did you ask him if he did it? Are you looking to start a fight? Excuse me, Little Miss Passive Aggressive, do you just want to be mad at him? (Rhetorical.) And let me start by saying, being "PA" is going to get you nowhere fast, trust me. …You *nag*.

Yes, you're a nag. You're the naggiest nag around and you know it! And so does the rest of the world because your man tells them all about it. (Trust me. You think he's not complaining about you? He is.) He leaves his plate in the sink for all of five minutes, you groan and wash it. His towel is on the floor in the bathroom and before he can even pick it up, you've done it, and bitched.

He hates you and it's all your fault!

I kid. Kinda.

Whatever, he's a pain in the ass.

Trust me, I get it! Still, you both have to fix this, or it will spiral out of control. As a coach, I can help, but the nagging and passive aggressive behavior must stop now, or he will end up shutting down and you will just resent him. Capiche?

You have very different communication styles: women are more active communicators; we tend to repeat ourselves. We tend to repeat ourselves. (Ha!) Over and over. We perseverate and obsess about things like rules or specific tasks we'd like done a certain way. This is so annoying and aggravating to men. (Hell, it's annoying to me. I'm actually annoying myself right now.)

And how do I know it's annoying? Oh, my boys have told me as much. Jim has told me; other guys have told me. Mark told me for most of my marriage … I go on and on about shit. My kids do this thing: when I say something more than once, they hold up two fingers. When I repeat it again, it's three fingers. And so-on. Well, screw you guys! Maybe if you'd just do the thing I asked you to do the first fucking time, I wouldn't have to repeat myself. I wouldn't have to repeat myself, damn it! So frustrating, right? Then when I ask them why they didn't do what I asked, they say, "We will, Mom. When we get to it. But you always do it anyway." This is so infuriating, because I want things done when *I want them done!*

I want things done on MY time; which is how it should be.

I have a message for you, ladies: *stop it!* Drop that dirty sock … and back away slowly.

Is that control worth your marriage?

Is it worth your relationship with your children?

The answer is *no.* It is not, and you have to stop it. Let the dirty sock lie precisely where it is, and he will pick it up. Now, it might not be at the time you'd like it to be done, or the way you'd like it to happen, but let it go. Learn to let the shit go! If he wants to help you fold towels and put them in the closet,

let the man fold them. Even if it kills you to watc
differently than how you usually do it.

Give him a chance; it shows him he is good enough.

Ahhhh … what was that, Jennifer?

He is *good enough?*

Yes, ma'am. He is good enough, and what he's capable of is enough. He has what it takes to do things just as well as you might do them. So, stop beating him up all the time over the mundane bullshit that is killing his self-esteem and bringing him down as a father and a man. Do you think he can't feed your kid or change a frickin' diaper? Back the fuck off, sister! Let that man make the mac and cheese! The doctor prescribed an antibiotic for your son, and you're not sure he is really capable of administering the correct dose? (Yah, well, me neither.) Step away from that syringe and give him a shot. (Pun totally intended.) What's the worst thing that happens? Your kid pukes from an overdose? He will live to see another day, and your hubby will never want to give him meds again.

Win-win!

He puts the reds in with the whites, so what?

Okay, actually no. This is where I step in and say HELL NO. I draw the line at mixing colors in the laundry. A woman has her limits, and this is my book after all. But honestly, your guy is enough; you married him for a reason. Whether he was going to be a good husband or a perfect father—or both! You picked him, now trust him! And show him you have a little faith.

Oftentimes, I hear from male clients that the nagging is too much to handle. What this really means is you are pressing a point, and he is withdrawing. Bad girl! Bad!

Both nagging and withdrawing are negative forms of communicating. If you keep pushing and he keeps shutting you down, eventually this will result in a blow up. Hello! You will feel as though he is ignoring your needs, while he feels like he's being "beaten up." Not a good scenario for either side and a horrible way to model communication skills for your children. You need to work together to find effective ways to talk to each other and resolve conflicts, as well. It's not only beneficial to fight fairly, but to know when to "make up" and end an argument the right way.

Conflict resolution is just as important as good communication.

I can remember when Mark and I used to make it a point to go to the boys and say, "Guys, we are okay. Mom and Dad were in a huge fight, but now we have made up." Okay, so they looked at us like we were freaks, but I felt like a really great parent. Mom of the year, really. It's the little things, y'all.

Peace Table.

Okay, here's another really great conflict mediation tip I love and used all the time in our house when the boys were younger. It's called the PEACE TABLE—and it works. Ready? Here's how it goes down.

Pick a spot in the main part of your house that is accessible to all parties and has some kind of empty table. It can be with or without chairs, doesn't matter. What does matter is that the kids (and you) can all fit around it and chat when there's a conflict to be resolved. So, when there's a fight breaking out, I would say, "Okay, boys! To the Peace Table!" They would stop in their tracks and run to the little plastic table and chairs in the play room. So cute, right? They would then take turns stating their "case." I always had a "wand" or some kind of gavel on the table too. So, they'd pass it back and forth and take turns talking. No talking when the other person is holding the "peace stick." (Okay, we didn't call it that, but you catch my drift.)

Lots of times, Mark and I would meet there for fun just to show the kids how to talk out our issues calmly and respectfully. Hey, I think I will bring back the Peace Table into my house now! Jonah and Zac will love it, no? To the Peace Table, men! Ha.

Now men, who are typically the more passive communicators, might have to take the lead when you start to nag. I know when I get "bitchy" and all up in my boyfriend's shit, he calmly and in a non-confrontational tone reminds me I need to "chill." Now, this is a very, very slippery slope. Most women do not like the words: "calm down," "chill out," "easy," "relax," or "breathe." So, choose your words carefully, boys!

Truth be told, when I start to get all riled up or naggy-nutty with my kids, they use a "safe-word" with me. I'm not kidding! Our word is "pineapple." All they have to do is say, "Pineapple!" and I start laughing. I realize then that I'm acting like a loon and I come back down to earth. It might work for you. Just chose a word, and when you hear it, you'll remember life is short, and nothing should ever be that big of a deal. A kind of "check yourself before you wreck yourself" word so-to-speak.

A FEW TIPS FOR NAGS
(AND A FEW FOR THOSE BEING NAGGED):

- *Just Do the Dang Thing.* Alright, naggies! If you're being nagged all the time, is there a reason? How about you just do the thing already? Try that out for size. If you're sick of your wife nagging about picking up your socks off the bathroom floor, try this: PICK UP YOUR FLIPPIN' SOCKS! Okay? Cool.

- *Walk this Way.* Try this, nags: let it go and walk away. If you see that towel he left behind, just pick it up (or leave it) and walk on by. Is it worth the nagging and fighting? No. Walk. On. By.

- *Nagging is Negative.* There is just nothing positive about nagging your spouse or kids. Nada. So, try to avoid it at all costs. Again, just walk away. Then, when you've calmed down and you can approach the situation later, try and have a conversation about it. "Honey, I really hate being a nag. I know you hate when I nag you ... but it's impossible when ...." Then tell him how you miss all the good times you have when the house runs smoothly and how much you appreciate all the GOOD stuff he does to help out. (Positive plus!)

- *Don't Take it Personally.* Don't give weight to that towel he doesn't pick up, or the dish he forgot to put in the dishwasher ... again. It's not that he doesn't care about you, that's not why he didn't do it. It may be he just doesn't give two shits about the thing. Don't get all up in arms or make it about you. He still loves you and his forgetting has zero bearing on your relationship.

HE SAID / SHE SAID.

And he said,
"I wish she would have stopped yelling at me all the time. I hated getting bitched at. And the worst thing about it ... she always did it at night. I was like, 'Umm, it's bedtime mother fucker. Why are you still talking?' Lol."

And she said,
"If he would have just done things without me asking, I wouldn't have been the naggy bitch he thought I was. It's a two-way street!"

And he said,
"Why do women always obsess about the same thing, on and on, over and over? I honestly stop listening after the first three words."

And she said,
"Sometimes I just pick up all my husband's dirty gym clothes and put them on his pillow. I don't even say a word. After that, he usually picks them up off the floor for at least a month or two!"

And he said,
"I want to reach up and put my hand over my wife's mouth, is that wrong?" He laughs.

And she said,
"I don't want to be a nagging bitch, but how else am I supposed to get the help I need around my house? No one listens to me!"

What If?

A Real Look at Divorce

Intro to Part Two

I am happy.
I am content.

I am good with where I am living, who I am dating, and the career I have. But if you had told me ten years ago that I would be doing all of this alone, I'd have said you were out of your fucking mind.

And if you told me I would have less money, fewer friends, and way more anxiety to boot, I'd even be more surprised. I always thought divorce looked different: I figured it wasn't as bad as everyone made it out to be, and I would surely be fine after the dust settled. I just knew I would feel better if I was out of my "lonely, sexless marriage." I mean, after all, "a loveless marriage is far worse than a divorce." Right? That's what everyone (therapists, family, friends) told me when I looked for advice, when I told them I was "unhappy" in my twelve-year marriage. And I'm not placing blame. *I* made my final decision to pull the plug and leave. We decided it was best for our family.

But …

Looking back, what the fuck did they really know? Any of them. My side; his side. The therapists, the attorneys. Not one of them divorced! Having never been through divorce, how could they have possibly had any clue? Of course, they wanted me to be "happy." And sure, they wanted what was best for me "under the circumstances." But did they actually know what divorce "looked" like, having never been through it themselves?

The answer is "no."

A hard fucking no.

It's comparable to a male obstetrician telling a pregnant woman what giving birth to her first child will really feel like. He can explain the pushing. The need for drugs. He will go over the breathing and the different things that might or might not happen during labor. But honestly, that woman has absolutely no idea what it's going to be like until the moment she feels that first contraction. ... Oh, but the doctor explained it! He told her (as she's screaming for the epidural and cursing her baby daddy) it wasn't going to be "that bad." Sure, Doctor McDouchey told her, but she has to go through the vag ripping, and the shitting on the hospital table before she can fully understand the true extent of the experience. (And yes, I went there!)

The same is true with divorce.

No one truly gets it unless they've been through it.

I can't go back. I can't now, and I don't want to.

I know it seems crazy, but I am happy! Happy-ish, anyway, and more importantly, my boys are thriving! I've got my groove back and I'm bat-shit crazy in love. See, there *is* life after divorce, y'all. It just comes with such a price. And again, I am no way saying anyone should stay in a disastrous marriage.

Hear me when I say this, I am pro-marriage,
but if divorce is inevitable, I believe in doing it
as amicably and respectfully as possible.

Now, listen to me carefully, okay?

If you're married (crossing my fingers you haven't pulled the plug yet) I would love to help you keep it that way! That is why this next part of the book is so dang important, alright? I'm about to give you a bullshit-free look into the life of a divorced woman. (Surprise, it's me!) And I'm hoping to scare the bee-jeezus out of you! Ha. Let's keep it real: if I'd had a book that honestly laid all this shit out back when I was flirting with my ex-boyfriends on Facebook and Mark was sleeping in the guest room, I'd never have signed those damn divorce papers. Come on, people! We have all been there. I'm here to stop you from making the biggest mistake of your life.

If I have the "secret sauce" to save your marriage, don't you want it? (Rhetorical.)

Excellent! Then pick your jaw up off the floor and turn the page. Take a gander at what your life will look like if you choose divorce over actually nurturing your marriage and putting in the effort necessary to create an everlasting, loving partnership.

Let's not let you become a Woulda. Coulda. Shoulda. That's my job.

Birds of a Feather

Okay, so let's start Part Two off with a bang!
Here's one of the BIGGEST shockers
I had when I got separated.
And this one stung quite a bit.

rust me, no one wishes it wasn't the truth more than me. This stat sucks THE BIG ONE, but it's a stat nonetheless, so let's take it for what it's worth.

Are you ready?

Research has shown that the social network of mothers tends to change dramatically after divorce, with some women losing almost 40% of their friends,[1] particularly if the friendships were formed during the marriage.[2]

Ugh! Can you believe that? Well, it actually makes me feel a little bit better, to be honest. At least I know it wasn't just me! But alas, this is the way it goes when you're divorced in a sea of married people. And it's not your fault, oh married ones, really. It's just the way shit goes down after you end things and become a single lady. Your social life drastically changes; coupledom is a thing of the past. And it happens so quickly, it's almost as if you were never even part of coupledom at all. I don't blame my old friends, I don't. It's hard to have a single gal in the group. It makes everything weirdly uncomfortable and uneven. And they did witness me going through the most challenging time of my life, why would they want to keep talking about it?

I didn't want to talk about it either; neither did my boys, trust me.

So, "single" becomes, ummm, "individual?"

It's so weird, the whole "vanishing friends" thing, but I get it. I just never expected it to change so drastically; the loss of my social life after my divorce. I became unmarried, and I lost my married friends. I missed them so much. But I couldn't be mad at them (I was so mad at them) for not missing me back. They had their routines, their husbands … and I had nothing to bring to the table.

Funny thing was I thought I still did….

Have lots to bring to the table, that is. It still breaks my heart that I apparently didn't. And the most bizarre thing? They didn't choose my ex either! I figured it would be either him or me. But statistics show that most groups of couples just find it easier to dump both people in a former pair. The Team Him/Team Her thing never really works out anymore. And here we thought we were making it so much easier for our friends by being such great co-parents. We figured if we got along, all our friends would at least want one of us, or maybe even keep each of us with the friend of our respective gender? But nope. We both got the axe.

Shit.

And the kids took the hardest hit of all.

I never, ever expected that to happen. Fuck! Not only did we lose all our friends, but slowly, one by one, the boys started to lose their pals too. It was gradual and less noticeable. At first I thought it was a socioeconomic thing; I didn't have the money I used to because of the divorce. Obviously, I took a significant hit, so maybe we just couldn't keep up? But no. Perhaps our new house was in a shitty part of town? After all, we had to move out of our big, beautiful home in the Quail Hollow Country Club area. (Who cares!) Nope, that wasn't it. Hmmm. I couldn't figure it out! It just couldn't get any worse. They didn't get invited to their friends' houses or pools anymore. And because Mark and I didn't go places as a couple, they didn't get asked on family trips, either.

The kids didn't get invited anywhere because of our divorce. Not only had the boys lost their parents and "family," now they were losing their friends and social life, as well.

We were no longer a family. And when you are a "divorced kid," you don't fit in the "married kids" group. Again, I get it, kinda. … Okay, I'm lying, I don't! I don't understand why our old friends can't still invite Jonah to dinner when they all go, even if I'm not there. I'll send money—they don't have to pay for him! Or why Zac can't still get invited to the lake house with the other guys and moms. Maybe it's because they think he would feel out of place? The worst is social media. They see all of their friends together anyway when they "Snap" or post "pix" on "Insta." I have tried to tell them it's not their fault; it's mine and Mark's. But it still doesn't make it any better.

Honestly, I wanted to die.

Our divorce had officially ruined our boys' social lives.

If I had known it was going to hurt them so much … OMG. If only I had known. I mean, would I have changed things? Woulda, coulda … this had to get better, right? (And five years later, it has, just so you know.) But for the first couple of years right after the divorce, it was awful. And it killed me.

For the longest time, I still tried to make sense of it all. I saw my friends' Facebook posts of concerts and girl's trips to the beach. I wondered why I hadn't been invited, why they didn't want me to be there. Then I realized it was difficult for them too. What would they say or ask me? How would I feel being around a group of married couples? They probably thought they were easing my pain by not inviting me.

My friends were right.

After time passed, I just became an afterthought, a person they saw at the pool, or in the carpool line. Now, I sit alone— or with Mark—when we go to the boys' games. We always exchange pleasantries with the married peeps, ask how the kids are doing. We want to say more, talk longer, but there really is no point. We no longer have very much in common. I think married people just kind of forgot I existed. Not on purpose, I'm no longer an everyday part of the couple-group anymore. It happened, and it's okay. These days when I run into my old friends, we find ourselves feeling oddly out of place. So, we walk away, just the three of us (me and the boys). Then we watch our old friends get in their cars—as families—and I always get this weird lump in my throat, even after all this time.

I just didn't expect any of this when I decided to get divorced.

I never even thought about it.

When I was contemplating my divorce, I thought about losing my married life, just not about losing my married friends.

Shit, I thought about the kids, the house, more significant issues. But losing my social circle and married friends? Never. I still miss the connections we had; the tribe of women with all our commonalities. But after five years of being single, I've found new ones. I've met women who are divorced and in the same boat as I am. It's different because we've bonded over our pain and hurt, and not because our kids are in school together or our husbands golf together on Saturdays at the club.

These new bonds are different, not better … just different.

I have friends now who understand my loneliness and loss. Friends who are dating again and having to put themselves out there in this crazy mixed-up world. Friends who can relate to the fear of uncertainty that comes with not having a husband to come home to each night, or fall asleep with at the end of the day. They get it when I have to fix a toilet all by myself or when I lose my shit over a bill I can't afford—yet again.

Divorced friends get it because they have lived it, and are constantly going through it.

They understand first-hand and don't have to pretend to know how I'm feeling. It's like we have this divorced-girl code. I can just sit down with a divorced woman, and she knows what kind of shit I've been dealing with; no matter where I am in the process, she just knows. We share the same pain and carry the same guilt in knowing our children are struggling and we are the cause. Even if they are having a great day or doing well, we have guilt that never goes away. And even when our conversations get uncomfortable, there is no judgment, no apology, because we can be who we are and not feel shame. Divorce is not a "bad word" when I'm with my unmarried friends. And no one is worried I'm going to steal their husbands either!

… Just the guy they met on Tinder last week.

Ha! I kid. Kinda. Now, dating after divorce is a whole other animal. Yikes. And a whole other chapter! (Not that any of you are dating … I hope! But I figured I'd fill you in on the *hell* that's dating after divorce, just in case you were thinking of jumping ship.) In fact, we can do that one next! Yes … let's talk about dating! Did someone say, "Swipe right?"

Ugh.

1. Albeck, S., & Kaydar, D. (2002). Divorced mothers. *Journal of Divorce & Remarriage, 36,* 111-138.
2. Rands, M. (1988). Changes in social networks following marital separation and Divorce. In R. M. Milardo (Ed.) *Families and Social Networks.* Newbury Park, CA: Sage.

The Dating (after Divorce) Game

Me: Shave what?
Him: *Pointing down* That.
Me: My ... "landing strip"?
Him: Welcome back to dating, lady.

When I was married, I think I shaved once a year. Okay, maybe twice. Summer, and then again if I had to wear a dress. ... Okay, that's a "Jenism." I shaved if I knew I was going to have sex. So, like four times a year. Ha!

After I got a divorce, I shaved every time I had a date. *What?* Yes, I'm serious! I never knew if it was going to end in a "hook-up," so I had to be prepared. ... And not just my legs. I shaved every damn part of my body that had hair. Why? Because men don't like fuzzy anymore, didn't you know? Hair is so 2010. I shaved my legs, my armpits, and then ... I shaved my vag.

Not just the bikini area, y'all. But the Entire. Fucking. Thing.

Yes, ladies, hair is out, and bare is in. Forget that a bald vagina looks like a prepubescent girl's, just do it. Most men seem to think it's "sexy and hot" and well, all the "rage." Including my guy. He actually looked at my perfectly shaved "soul patch" with utter disgust. "What is that?" he said. I was like, "Ummm, it's a soul patch, duh!" He was like, "Why do you need that tiny little puff of hair? Just shave it all off!" I was stunned. No man before him had seemed to mind my cute little poof of hair. And I was sort of attached to it. I mean even if it was small and cute—and didn't serve much purpose—it was enough to make me a *woman* for fuck's sake.

So, I kept my Soul Patch Poof (SPP) for the first three months we dated. He was so grossed out, but I didn't care. I stood my ground and told him if he didn't like the hair on my vag, he didn't have to go there! He laughed. We laughed. And then on Valentine's Day, I surprised him. YES! I shaved off the little poof! (TTYL, SPP!) And guess what? He didn't even notice.

He didn't fucking notice!

But I just stood there in the mirror, looking like a twelve-year-old girl. Or one of those hairless cats. What are they called? Ummm … Mr. Bigglesworth? Dr. Evil would have loved this pussy, y'all. Yesss! (And Millennials, if you didn't get the reference to *Austin Powers,* it's okay. Just drink a La Croix and relax.) I looked like a newborn fucking gerbil … I was beside myself.

And he didn't even care ….

Or at least he didn't "use his words." I expected a huge reaction; after all, I thought this was a big deal. I guess it wasn't, because men just expect hairless lady bits these days. Ugh. Over are the days of the disco-porn-bush and grown out pubes! Invest in a Costco supply of razors or a monthly package of Brazilians at your favorite European waxing place—you're going to need them. Or, if you like your "womanhood" and want to keep your landing strip, make sure it's cleaned up and nicely groomed. Some men, and I'm saying "some" lightly, are into the hairy bush. But trust me, they will not admit it until you're lying naked with the lights out. He will whisper quietly, "I'm totally low-key into that soul-patch." Oh, and if he does admit he likes it, he's most likely under the age of thirty.

… Not that I would have any personal experience! (Psst, I'm forty-six, can you say cougar?)

Just doing my research, y'all. Doing my research and here's what I've found:

THE BOTTOM LINE ON HAIR "DOWN THERE."

Men don't complain as long as:
- They can see what they're looking at (the forest through the trees).
- It's groomed and pretty, sans rash and bumps preferred.
- It don't stank! (Feminine hygiene is important, ladies!)

And just be prepared for coming upon (pun intended) men with perfectly manscaped pubes, as well. It threw me for quite the loop! I was married for twelve years and boy have things changed in the world of men and manscaping! The "manzillian" is just as popular for men as Brazilian waxing is for the ladies! Wowza. Let's just say getting intimate after divorce is *much* different than being with a man you trusted and had a deep connection with for years. In fact, it's downright petrifying! Yo, married mamas, are you ready to show your lady-bits for a stranger again? Yah, not so much? (Little thought nugget for ya.)

I will never forget the mixed emotions I had getting naked that first time for a man who wasn't my wasband. I mean, Mark knew my body. My imperfections. My likes; dislikes. What the fuck was I doing? It was uncomfortable, but exciting. Scary, but thrilling. I had so many emotions. I remember excusing myself and going into the bathroom, turning on the fan … and crying into a towel. I was sobbing, thinking, "What are you doing, Jen?" A man I didn't even know was touching me.

… A man I didn't even know was touching me?

Wow. A man I didn't even know was touching me!

Let that sink in, then read it one more time. OMG. Do you know what I'm getting at? You have to take off your clothes, and let a man see you naked for the first time, *all over again.* And again, and then again. It's called dating after divorce.

This so-called "dating after divorce" is a whirlwind of emotions. The question really is: when are you ready to process those emotions? And are you in the right headspace to act accordingly when you have to deal with rejection, the craziness of online communication, and all the other bullshit that's thrown at you? Ask yourself, are you ready to become emotionally—and physically—connected to someone again?

There are so many things that need to happen before you begin this intimate process of loving and trusting. So many things!

Remember dating before you got married?
Yah, dating after divorce looks NOTHING like that!

Lookey, cookie: dating after divorce *sucks.* And if you do it too soon, *ugh.* I did it way too soon, and some coaches (including me) will say to wait one year after your separation to even think about dating. But then there are others that say everyone is different and each divorce is different. "You'll know when you know." What a crock of shit. YOU NEED A YEAR. And this is the one thing I wish I had listened to my therapist about. Why didn't I? Because I thought I knew it all, of course. But after a divorce you are so fucked up, you know nothing.

And married people, you too know nothing—no offense. (Stay out of it. Ha.) I used to love my married friends and family telling me I was "dating too many people," or, on the other hand, I needed to "get out there and stop feeling sorry for myself." Really? Pick one! Should I stay home and wallow in self-pity, or fuck everything that moves? Yeesh. How about this: I just lost my family, my house, my life ... and I have NO idea which end is up! I digress, but a *full year* after a divorce is the most difficult. So, please wait at *least* that long until you date anyone seriously.

Personally, I was like, "No, screw that, not me!" I honestly thought I could date like I used to before I was married. It would be like "back in the day," ya know? I'd get fixed up by a friend or meet a guy at a party and I'd give him my number. What is this, 1997? *Whoooaaa, Missy.*

Welcome to Online Dating 101: cyber hell. Did you know guys don't even talk to you in person anymore? Yah, G-d forbid they make too much eye contact. What a shonda! It's all texting and shit. Oh, and there's like an app for everything. Buzzing, swiping, beeping, matching, and fishing? WTF? Can't we just talk on the phone all night and make mixed tapes? Nope. *Slllooowww your roll, bitches.* Dating is a whole new ball game.

And as far as dating was concerned ... I did everything wrong, even though it felt so right.

Take the time you need to get yourself emotionally stable and your kids in a safe, healthy environment. I jumped into a relationship and I wasn't prepared for the shit show that was dating after divorce. I wish so badly I could go back and erase that "stupid-ass mistake." (Name withheld because he doesn't deserve a plug!) I introduced him to my kids, I met his. We went on vacations and posted pictures on social media. He was my very first "love" after my twelve-year marriage … but I wasn't his first. I was his third or fourth girlfriend. And I was disposable. He broke up with me after six months, and I was devastated. Alone and heartbroken—again.

It was honestly worse than my divorce, because I was prepared for *that* breakup. That one was talked about and discussed in detail. I had a part in it, and it was partly my own decision. This one was not. I was dumped, and the guy didn't give much of a shit. It set me way, way back and my kids had to go through another "man" leaving us.

And they had to see Mommy crushed.

Allowing the kids to meet a man too soon after divorce is not good for anyone, or anything. If you ever are in this position, take the time you need to get healthy and happy with yourself, before you even think about introducing those kids to anyone of the opposite sex. (Or the same sex if that's your preference.) Just no "meets" until everyone is ready—no matter who you choose to be with! ;)

The first relationship out of the gate NEVER works, people. And if it does, it will not last for long. It. Never. Lasts.

I have since taken the time to do the self-healing and exploration I needed from the start, and now I coach women (and men) like myself on how to do divorce right. If you have to get divorced, you bet your ass I'll help you do it as amicably and respectfully as possible. I do believe in "Happy Divorce," as long as you put your kiddos first and leave your ego at the door. I've got you all covered: married, I'll help keep you that way; divorced, I'm here to talk you through it. It's the best of both worlds. In my humble opinion (IMHO), who wouldn't want a divorce coach telling you how to stay married? I know how to fix what I fucked up.

Boom!

So, yes, when it comes to dating after a divorce, there is a "too soon," there are rules to "online dating success," and there are foolproof methods to make this shit easier! I am in a healthy, happy relationship now ... after four years of self-exploration. I'm a big advocate of self-love and taking care of your head and heart. And boy have I done some major work on me. Divorce is painful, we all know that. You have to heal. That's why I like to tell newly divorced peeps who I coach, even if you think you've got it all together, and you're ready to hop on a dating site, take a deep breath ... and then wait two more months. Time is your best friend; use it!

Let's say you do get separated. Yes, *you.* (FYI: In some states, dating is allowed during the separation period; in others, it's not.) ... Can you even imagine starting all over with a new person? What would you look for this time around? Where would you even begin? Would you pick someone with the same qualities you were attracted to in your spouse, or steer clear of every single characteristic he possessed? Yah, never crossed your mind, right? Never crossed mine either, until it had to. It can be exciting! But also, nerve-racking.

Now, at this point in your life (if you already have kids), you may not be looking for a good father or great provider, but just searching for a solid person. *Phew!* Keep in mind, the most "solid" of guys will still have baggage, and lots of it. His baggage will have to fit with your baggage.

Cool, let's unpack all that baggage. He will have an ex and a story. He might have kids, and live in a certain part of town, and he might have a totally different schedule. Religion, race, age … all factors to consider. Oh, and he has herpes? And a cat, OMG I hate cats.

Isn't dating post-divorce fun? I'm schvitzing just thinking about it!

And on the flip side, why be so picky? Maybe this guy is just for shits and giggles. Or just for sex. *OMG, Jen, really?* Yes, really. Imagine after twenty-plus years of marriage you get to "pick" anyone you want out of hundreds of men online. You don't have to stay in any relationship that doesn't fit your emotional, physical, or spiritual needs. You can get out anytime you want. … But guess what? So can he. No ring; no commitment. *Oh, wow. He can just* dump *me anytime? FUCK. What if I dig him and I feel a real connection?* So what, Buttercup! He has a date next week with some other chick he met on Tinder.

Did I mention dating after divorce totally sucks? ;)

I remember when I was contemplating separation and thinking about having to date again. I thought how fun it would be to "get back out there" and have someone actually pay attention to me, or say kind things. I get it, y'all. That temptation is real. I also remember thinking I'd have it easy.

(Ha.) Others warned me divorce was a mess and the "dating pool" was filled with married men and guys with more baggage than the airport, but I didn't care. Jennifer Hurvitz would be a-okay! *Bring on the dating after divorce*, I thought, and let's hop the fence to that greener-grass called freedom!

Four years(ish), eight "real" relationships, fifty-plus dates, one shaved vagina, and a few psychopaths later ... (umm ... did I jump the wrong fucking fence?) ...

... And *finally*, I'm with the man I love and *deserve*. Oh, and he loves me back! (Yah!) So, there's that. And it's not easy, not even a little bit. (That chapter is coming.) It has been a nightmare, this "finding the man I love thing" and making it work with our current situations. Are you reading this, people? Do you like the pajamas you're wearing and the comfortable feeling you have snuggled up next to that guy you've known since college? (Even if he farts.) And isn't it nice to get undressed and not feel judged? Or to have conversations only the two of you understand? Or to not wear makeup or blow-dry your hair and still feel wanted (even if sometimes you don't want it!)?

You get my point, right? I am in love, yes. But Holy Hell, Batman! It has been exhausting. That's just part of divorce. If you ever find yourself in my shoes, you will fail miserably. *I* failed miserably. You will make mistakes, over and over. I made too many to count. Just like marriage, divorce takes work. All relationships take work. People take work, for fuck's sake!

Don't beat yourself up.

Dating after divorce can (and will) be successful if you start with the right attitude, and at the correct time.

Be strong, be brave, and be BADASS.

Whether you're married, in a relationship, separated, or divorced, practice self-love. It's okay to sit with your emotions and do absolutely nothing until you are ready to make a decision. Just breathe. Take the time you deserve; the time your children need. Then breathe some more. Or just call a friend, grab a bottle of good wine, and watch Netflix.

Who needs all this crap, anywho? I say, love the one you're with.

Woulda. Coulda. Shoulda. ;)

Shock Waves

He moves out.
You sign the papers.
Wow.

Imagine it with me: you're legally separated. Now what?

I wish someone *would have* told me just how badly it would hurt. Yah. Even though I wanted to be separated, and so did Mark. We had talked about it for months, years ... never had a blowout fight, we were amicable as two people could be. So, why did it still hurt that bad?

I was shocked.

I was shocked by the pain, the overwhelming feeling of loss and sadness.

It felt like I had lost my best friend, lover, and family all in one fell swoop. The grief was devastating and I found myself crying more often than I ever imagined I would. I'd have days that were normal, days where I felt fine. Then there were days I couldn't get out of bed. Usually, the good days coincided with when I had the boys, and the bad days were when they were with Mark, of course. I missed my babies so much, and I remember my chest hurting when Mark would take them from my house on Friday nights. Jesus, why didn't anyone tell me it would hurt that badly?

It was crushing.

And the funny thing? The pain never had to do with missing Mark or wanting to be back with him; instead, it was the realization that I had to completely start over with my life. That was the biggest shock for me.

I had to come to grips with going back to square one and beginning my life as a single person all over again—only this time with two young boys.

Every time I left the house, it felt like people were looking at me differently. (Now I'm sure they weren't.) But I was paranoid. My hands looked so bare without my rings, so I went to a jewelry store and bought a cute one to wear just so they didn't feel "naked." I would drive past our old house and cry, wondering if the new family liked it as much as we had. I'd wonder if they'd painted the rooms new colors, how they'd set up the back porch. Stupid, but I just kept thinking about my old life.

I never expected it to hurt the way it did, or for so long.

But it did.

And then … it didn't.

And then it did, all over again. And the hurt was sometimes replaced with loneliness. Emptiness and sadness. I saw a therapist and continued to take my medication for depression and anxiety. It helped. Kinda. But the craziest thing? I had felt alone in my marriage too. And I oftentimes had said to Mark, "If I'm going to feel this alone, I might as well just *be alone* and reap the benefits." (Ha.) The benefits? What the fuck was I talking about? What benefits did I think came with a divorce? Ohh … right, the ones I saw in movies and heard about from my many divorced friends. You do know misery loves company, right? There was this imaginary picture I made up in my head, this "la-la land" of what alone and divorced would or *should* look like. Ya know, I'd have so much free time to do new things, to "find myself" again. I could start dating and be the woman I always wanted to be ….

Right.

Alone and married is nothing like alone and divorced. Nothing.

And to be honest, when married women say shit to divorced women like, "Why don't you just get out and do something?" or "You have all the free time in the world; I'm so jealous!" it is hard not to slap them. When was the last time you ate dinner alone or spent two weeks, or a *month* completely by yourself? "Alone" and married, you still have your family around you twenty-four/seven. Alone and married, you still have a person next to you every night (even if you're not making love as much as you'd like). Alone and married you get to *choose* when you want to be alone, you get that, right? It's a *choice*. You can choose to go on a girl's trip, or take a bath, or go out with your friends. But when you get back from being by yourself, you are not alone. You have your kids and your husband. Your family.

Alone and married may not be "healthy" or "perfect," but it can be FIXED if you BOTH put the time in to find your way back.

Alone and married is more like lonely than actually alone. Do you know what I mean? (And again, if you're in an abusive, horrific marriage, I'm not saying to stay.) I'm sure at this point so many of you are screaming at the book right now, saying,

"But as a divorced woman, *you* can make the best out of your situation, Jennifer!"

And you're right.

And I did. And I do. I *try.* I try to get out lots and travel on my off-weeks. I write and spend time with my boyfriend and my single friends. The aloneness isn't always around in the forefront of my life, but it lingers, quietly. And sure, I may seem pessimistic, but I'm not. I'm being honest. And yes, I'm crying as I write this, even though I am in a fabulous place and my life is good, because my house is *so quiet* ... and my boys are with their dad. I am by myself this weekend.

In all my research I have learned that this feeling of aloneness is not a bad emotion to have. It's not unhealthy. It's not, really. Being lonely—or alone—reminds us that we "want" others and "need" them to want us in return. *Sigh.* See? I'm not so messed up after all. :)

One of the big questions I'm often asked by my clients is, "*How long will it take me to get over my divorce?*" Well, unfortunately this is a toughie, because as I've said before, every divorce is different. Divorces come with their own unique set of circumstances and characteristics, as do marriages. Even if you have an amicable separation, you could have your own individual issues with the process that another person just may not have. One person might take years to resolve the pain of the divorce; the other, no time at all. In my experience and from research, I've found there are factors that can truly affect how long it will take to recover from a divorce:

Factors that Affect Divorce Recovery Time.

What type of marriage did you have? Let me go deeper. Did y'all end this thing on good terms? Was it amicable or not? Are the kids doing "okay" or is it a hot mess? Can you be in the same room without killing each other? All of this plays into the grieving process and the recovery.

When did you start mentally preparing for your divorce? Did you dream about dumping your spouse, or was this dropped on you like a bomb? Did you talk about it for years and decide together it just was time to move on? Or did he walk in one day and say, "I'm in love with my college girlfriend"? This will make a huge difference in how fast you can move on.

Who left whom? This plays one of the biggest factors in all the recovery shit. Who was the "dumper" and who was the "dumpee"? Yikes. No one likes to get kicked to the curb, so unless this was a mutual decision, someone always ends up way ahead in the recovery process.

Support system set to go? Do you have help? Do you have a solid support system ready to go and be there for your emotional needs? I'm not talking about a family member to kick you while you're down. I'm talking about a divorce coach to give you unbiased, non-judgmental opinions about all things divorce. It's so important to move forward fast and a divorce coach will speed the process along by not allowing you to wallow in self-pity for too long. He or she can provide you with coping tools, and help you set goals and move along in the grieving process so you can lay this thing to rest.

It's been years, and still I can't wait until each Monday after school when I get the boys back. It never surprises me how much I've missed their faces. Never, ever. But … I have learned it is okay to be alone! Think of the perks: You get to watch what you want on TV, you can eat whatever the hell you choose, and you can fart! You can fart anytime you want! That is the best reason to be alone, ladies. Being able to pass gas. Hehe!

Woulda. Coulda. Shoulda.
Pfttt. Oh, pardonne moi! ;)

Happy Holidays?

Ahhhh, it's that time of year again ...
CHRIS-A-KAH!
(Or is it Han-a-mas?) Whatever!

The stores are packed with busy shoppers. Yards covered with inflatable Santas, snow globes, and other enlarged holiday favorites. Kids everywhere are making their holiday "wish lists," and parents are stressing about getting exactly what's on them.

Holidays are crazy, stressful, and sometimes overwhelming. The holidays are that time of year when even the easiest of tasks causes us to lose our guts. Have you been to Target pre-Christmas on a Sunday? Even the calmest of women have been known to lose their shit in aisle three. (Yah, that's me.) So, if you are lucky enough to have a partner-in-crime to alleviate the pressure a bit, awesome! It's always nice to share the undue stress of the holidays with your mate. Marriage is good that way!

But what if you were divorced?
Bah-fucking-humbug.

Can you imagine handling an entire holiday on your own? Sans a hubby or wife? Can you even imagine being alone on Christmas morning or not having your kids with you on the first night of Hanukkah? How about knowing a *year* in advance that you will not be with your child for the upcoming Christmas Eve ... a family tradition you've spent together for the last twelve years? Or maybe Thanksgiving will be spent with *his* side this year, not yours? Yikes.

I have spent so many holidays over the last five years solo, or without my kids. I've even spent a few with someone else's kids, which is sometimes even more difficult. It sucks when you are lighting the menorah with your boyfriend's children, fully wishing you were with yours, but trying so hard to be happy in the moment. Or how about when the kids are with your ex on the beach in Florida and you're home, eating latkes from Poppy's Bagels? Alone. In your pajamas. Or athleisure wear (I chuckle) and Uggs. Looking at your phone. Waiting for pics.

Being divorced around the holidays can be one of the hardest things to handle. I mean, where do I even start? *I know,* we asked for it when we got divorced, right? Well, some of us did. Others, not so much. I have girlfriends who never asked to be cheated on or left for another man. Or guy friends who didn't expect their wives to come home with the kids' karate instructor. Those same friends never expected to be eating Christmas Eve dinner alone at The Great Wall of China. There is nothing fun about divorce, people. Not. One. Thing.

Phew. With that said, I do have a few Helpful Hints

for a Happy (and Healthy) Holiday that I think might be beneficial. I know they help me get through that time of year. Even though it's never easy, it can be better … *ish*. And married folks, just consider it a peek with the Ghost of Christmas Future, if you were to be divorced. Or maybe you have a divorced friend that could use your help during the holidays; take notes … and give them a jingle.

HURVITZ'S HELPFUL HINTS FOR A HAPPY (AND HEALTHY) HOLIDAY

Be prepared. Okay, this sounds silly, but it's an excellent tip! Prepare yourself for what's coming, guys. If you know you're not going to have your kiddos on Christmas next year because you chose to do alternating years for holidays, plan ahead! Make plans for you. Go on a trip. A great trip! Plan a trip to Europe with other divorced peeps. Save all year and just go. You will be sad, you will be lonely, and you must be prepared for it. Or, plan to spend the holiday with your family and friends to celebrate.

I spent one year in Maui with my entire family when my boys were with my ex. Did I miss them? Hell yes. But I missed them way less on the beach! Ha. Do not sit home alone. Go have fun and relish the fact that your kids are enjoying themselves just as much.

Home alone. Do not, I repeat, DO NOT ever sit home alone and wallow in your self-pity. Get up and get out. I don't give a rat's patootie what you do, just do something other than sit. Sitting is not good for you, or your tushie. Go take a yoga class or serve dinner to the homeless. (This will also make you feel good.) Or better yet, start a new hobby that gets you out of the house. Just get up and get your ass out of the house. Holiday

CONTINUED ON NEXT PAGE

time is not the time to binge The Sinner on Netflix. (... Although it is fucking fantastic. And Married at First Sight did keep me happy at home this past Christmas season while my kids were at the Michigan Bowl Game. Just saying!)

Be flexible. Plans (and custody arrangements) can be flexible if you and your ex are effectively co-parenting and well-behaved. Listen, rules are made to be broken. There is nothing wrong with celebrating a holiday together if the kids are okay with it. I'm not saying you move in for the weekend, but who's to say you can't go over for Christmas dinner and leave after? I bet the kids would love it, and it shows them you are capable of acting like grown-ups too. And if you have alternating years for holidays, there is no reason you can't change it to splitting the day instead. Try sharing Christmas where one of you takes Christmas Eve, the other Christmas Day. Hanukkah has eight crazy nights! You take four, your ex takes four. Get it? I feel strongly that kids deserve to see both parents every year.

Tradition! And yes, I'm singing that in my best Tevye voice. Look, you will miss the usual traditions you had as a family, I get it. Trust me, I do. But it's your job to make new ones. Instead of having Christmas morning with all of you making hot chocolate and opening gifts, maybe it's time to change it up. Try doing something off-the-wall and entirely wacky! I took my kids to look at Christmas lights one year (we are Jewish), and they thought it was really cool. Just because I could. And I got a little tree and put blue and silver balls on it and a Star of David on top. (Just because I could.) And it wasn't to spite my ex ... it was so we could have something different and unique in our house. They loved it and have since outgrown it (they are fifteen and sixteen now), but I loved seeing them smile. Tradition!

> **Just eat it.** Get that one thing (or three) you have been craving all year. And enjoy it. Open a great bottle of wine and just indulge. You actually get to be alone on a holiday! No stress, no family, no fighting! Don't think of it as negative; flip it into a positive. You. Are. Alone. Wine and good food ... maybe a nice bath. I bet there's not a married woman reading this who doesn't wish she could have one Christmas Eve to herself. Just once. Enjoy!

Divorce sucks any time of year. (Sorry, it's the truth.) Unfortunately, the holidays tend to suck a little bit more. I wish I could lie and say otherwise, but this girl is not into reindeer games!

The Truth about Co-parenting

No two divorces are ever the same.
They're like thumbprints, or snowflakes ...
shitty, melty snowflakes ...
each has their own individual characteristics.

One divorce could have kids involved, the other, none. Or maybe one person cheated or fell in love with someone outside of the marriage. Often times, one person wants out of the relationship, while the other is fighting desperately to make it work. Some get over our breakups quickly, and others take years to move on. Whatever the case, divorces are unique in their own way, which is why trying to understand someone's personal situation is so tricky.

Some people have beautiful relationships with their exes, and others can't even be in the same room, or breathe the same air.

People try so hard to compare their relationships (or former relationships) to others, giving examples of friends or coworkers. But other relationships never really are precisely the same as yours, are they?

And then, as if divorce isn't stressful enough, you might have children to add into the mix. There are thousands of different ways to divide schedules between parents. There's the week-on, week-off; the two-two-five; the week with one and weekends with the other; and the list goes on and on .... Everyone feels it's necessary to add their two cents into this as well. "Oh no, you should do the two-two-five, it's best for their stability," or, "You have got to do week-on, week-off if you want them to be okay!"

And the truth of the matter is, if you choose to divorce, they will never really be "okay."

Yes, I said that.

And yes, you can close this book if you want to; write me hate mail. But you know I'm right. Divorce causes permanent damage and trauma that we cannot reverse. (Well, unless you never get divorced at all. But sometimes the divorce is necessary.) Ugh! What a mess. And unfortunately, the adverse effects of divorce can be long-lasting on children and may impact their own relationships later in life. "Studies have shown that in the US, the daughters of divorced parents have a 60% higher divorce rate than those of non-divorced parents. The number is 35% for sons."[1] While there are short-term effects such as anxiety, mood swings, irritability, and extreme sadness, there are also many long-term effects as well (behavioral and social problems, substance abuse, and depression to name a few).

Recently, I had my boys Jonah (sixteen) and Zac (fifteen) on my podcast, *Doing Divorce Right,* as guests.

I was so excited; I couldn't wait to interview them and talk about how well-adjusted and happy they had become since the divorce in 2014. I mean, after all, their dad and me did it right! We did the "nesting" thing for as long as we possibly could. (Ya know, nesting? Where the kids stay in the family home, and the parents move out and get an apartment? Then, every other week the mom or dad switches in and out, instead of the children moving back-and-forth between two different homes. It's supposed to be a "warm-up" of sorts and make for an easier transition.) We made a solid pact to put our egos aside and put the boys first; we never fought in front of them, and we are truly best friends.

But you know what happened when I asked my boys what they thought the best thing about our divorce was? When I asked what we did *right* when it came to the divorce?

Zac said, "Well, Mom. The best way to divorce is to not get divorced at all."

I was live. On air. And I almost threw up. Here I was thinking the guys were "happy" and doing well. I mean, they are ... I think. I asked him to go on and tell me honestly how he felt. He said, "The nesting *sucked*. It was horrible. We hated being in our house while you and Dad switched in and out." Jesus Christ! Could the kid make me feel like a bigger piece of shit? Here I was thinking we had done the best thing for them! In my first book, I talked about nesting as being one of the most selfless things a parent can do for their kids! And my kids HATED it? I lived in a fucking apartment with MY EX for nine months and left my boys in the house so they could get more adjusted to divorce! I mean, doesn't that sound like the best possible plan?

Then Jonah pipes in, "Mom, you thought at the time it was a great idea, but it just wasn't. You should've ripped off the Band-Aid, okay?" Ugggggghhhh!

Woulda. Coulda. Shoulda!

Look, Zac also said he never heard Mark and me fight when we were married, so the divorce was a total and complete shock to him. And Jonah told the world how he lost all his friends because of us. Shit.

Still, if I could go back, would I? No. They *are* happy despite what they said that day, trust me. And I want them to see a loving, healthy relationship and be able to be great boyfriends and husbands because of it. But shit did that sting. It was an eye-opening podcast if I do say so myself.

I guess there have been a plethora of "eye-openers" involving co-parenting that I wish I would've known before I got divorced. You know, before I thought it was going to be so "happy" and perfectly perfect all the time. Look, I wasn't naïve. Or stupid. I gave hours upon hours of thought to the "normal" issues I would face: the division of property; sharing the kids week on, week off … and the loneliness. But what never even crossed my mind were the little things, the day-to-day feelings and minutiae that popped up out of nowhere and caught me by surprise! Why didn't anyone warn me? Why did nobody tell me I'd wonder what Jonah was thinking when I wasn't with him, or what the doctor had said about Zac during Mark's week?

Yes, co-parenting is easier when you get along. When everyone is flexible and kind, you respect each other and put the *kids* first.

But it still wasn't what I thought it would be.

My "Happy Divorce" has been filled with
lots of not-so-happy stuff.

The guilt never ends. Period. End of story. From the second
I looked into my children's eyes and told them their dad and
I were splitting up, I felt guilty. I still feel enormous guilt for
my decision, and I know Mark feels the same. And now, this
guilt carries over into just about every decision I make as a
single mom. I want them to be well-adjusted, happy, and live
the life they "used to have." I took it all away from them so I
could live a "happier life"? Fuck. I'm crying as I type this. And
I will never, ever forgive myself no matter how many times I
say, "Oh, they are so much better off seeing me happy." As far
as I'm concerned, that's just a bullshit thing divorced parents
say to make ourselves feel better for fucking up our kids' lives.
Come on, are they genuinely happier being split between two
houses, going back and forth, and living without both of their
parents? Rhetorical. But I say, not. (Unless of course, they
were in a home with drugs, alcohol, or abuse. Or if the two
of you just couldn't stop fighting in front of them, or it was
too hostile of an environment. Then, they are much better off
with a divorce.)

Personally? I will never stop feeling guilty. Never.

3's a Crowd. My most favorite part of co-parenting:
triangulation! That's when the kid plays the parents against
each other, and it works! Ha. My kids used to be the best
at this until Mark and I put the kibosh on it, and our lives
became much happier. DO NOT let your kids play this game.

Jonah once said, "Well, Dad said you are the worst cook
and no wonder we are sick all the time!" Ummm, OMG.

"Did he say that, Jonah?" I asked as I reached for my phone to text Mark and give him a piece of my mind. "Mark, did you tell the boys they get sick all the time because I can't cook? What the FUCK?" (Jonah, at this point, was nowhere to be found.)

"Jen," Mark replied, "I never said that, but Jonah told me you said I don't give them their vitamins—and I do! So, I can't understand why you are bad-mouthing me to them."

And so on, and so on. And it just kept getting worse and worse. But … Jonah got his parents to talk and communicate, do you see? Aha! Communication is good. But no, triangulating is not good … for anyone.

Instead, try mom and dad being on the same team even though you are parenting in different homes. Show the kids that even though you do not make a good couple anymore and can't get along in the same house, you can still function as a team and work together. Do not allow the kids to pull this bullshit.

No triangulating!

Home alone. If you ask me where I'm going to be next Fourth of July, 2020, I can tell you. Or if I have the kids for Christmas next year. I know right now. Divorced peeps usually have their holiday schedules all mapped out years in advance. And some co-parenting plans even do the holidays year on, year-off. Works out for lots of folks. My ex and I still utilize the week on, week off no matter what. So, whenever a holiday falls during my week, I get the boys. Make sense? This also means I am home alone for many of them. And it totally sucks.

At the beginning of our separation, we spent the big Jewish holidays together, mainly because we live in Charlotte and have no family here. Plus, the boys needed to see us still coming together as an "unfamily." But now, five years out, we divide and conquer, and it's great, but not so great when one of us is left solo. Yikes. It's pretty hard celebrating Valentine's Day without my boys when I know they are probably doing nothing at Mark's house. We have traditions over here, with candy and cards, but when I don't have them, well … it sucks, ya know? It's just not the same the next day.

Baby of mine. And how about when it's the kid's actual birthday, and you don't have him? OMG, I birthed the damn child, and I can't be with him on his birthday? This year was Jonah's sixteenth. *His sixteenth fucking birthday!* … And he was with his dad. In fucking amazing Seattle. Fun, right? Yah! So fun. I can't afford to take him, so Mark got to be Dad of the Year. Doubly shitty. I called Jonah and tried so hard not to cry. This was the very first birthday I didn't see him or kiss him. The very first one since he was born.

Divorce fucking sucks.

Control freak. I'm pretty type A. (I think most women are, right?) Well, most moms I know like structure—and so do their kids. Imagine having ZERO control over anything in your child's life. Like nada. Zilch. Nothing.

You've just imagined co-parenting! Yikes, right? I drop the boys off at Mark's house every other Friday afternoon, and from that point forward, he has complete control over every single thing they do for the next week. If he wants to let them stay up all night, they do. If they're going to watch R-rated movies, done deal. Whatever *he* chooses to do as the custodial parent for the week is *his* decision; I can't even bat an eyelash. Oh, like the time I got a call from Zac after Mark took him to this "fancy place" for dinner and he ate bone marrow. He gave my nine-year-old fucking *bone marrow* ... and kangaroo meat. Yah, zero control, people. (You still want to get divorced? Ha.)

Now, I am lucky. Mark is a rockstar dad; he parents much like I do. Phew. But how about a dad who has no clue? Or a dad who doesn't even try to follow the mom's rules or suggestions? How about a parent (either a dad or mom) who won't even return a phone call or a text for the entire time he or she has the kids? Fuck, guys. I have the best divorce of most I've seen ... I cannot imagine co-parenting with a person who doesn't involve me in my kids' lives. But, news flash: it happens more often than not. I have friends who have to pray their kids come back alive every time they drop them off, for reals. One time a guy friend of mine left his daughter with his ex-wife and she gave their ten-year-old a Xanax ... "by accident." Not quite sure how that happened, but it did. Suffice it to say, they ended up in front of a judge. See, it's not always the divorced dads who are the issue! Moms fuck up too.

Role reversal. I was the stay-at-home mom. (Hey, SAHMs!) I had the job of raising my boys, taking care of the house, and blah blah blah. You know the drill. Mark, on the other hand, had a significant role at the bank. He busted his ass every day and did the "dad stuff." Ya know, the bills, the car, the house shit? Boy do I wish I learned how to do that dad shit, and I'm pretty dang sure he wishes he had a better handle on the mom crap!

Do you know what a huge shock it was when I started living all alone as a single mom? Holy HandyMan, Hurvitz! Does anyone know how to change a lightbulb? (I kid ... kinda.) I had no clue how to do anything conventionally "man-ish." Now I'm not being sexist here. I'm also talking about shit like the lawn, killing animals that show up in the dark, changing car parts ...

and if you ladies can do all that or even love to do it, AMEN! You go, girls! But for me? Not a chance. And when it was late at night, and I heard a noise in the attic or in the garage, I missed Mark! I missed having a man in my house, even if I wanted to kick his ass most of the time. It took a lot of getting used to being a single mom *and* the dad of the house. My boys had to step up and help out, especially when I started working, too. Yeesh. Oh, how things did change.

Did you know Jonah can fix a toilet? (Okay, almost fix a toilet.) Just last week I found him upstairs with the top off the dang thing playing with the lever, trying to make it fill back up with water or some craziness. We ended up calling Jim over in the end, but I was pretty impressed Jonah even tried. He said, "I've got this, Mom. I'll save you money so you don't have to call a plumber!" Sweetest damn thing. Oy.

Now, over at my ex's house, things were just as bad if not worse!

Can you imagine what a total shock being a single dad and a mom was to his system? He not only had to go to work forty-plus hours-per-week (and travel), but now he also had to take care of two teenagers all by himself. Laundry, cooking (not that I ever used to cook, ha!), cleaning the house, packing lunches … OMG, poor thing. It was tough for him. The boys tried to help, but for him it was a much slower adjustment. I found myself at his house several times, straightening up and helping out. After all, my kids had to live there.

Quiet, please. When I was married, I always wanted my boys to shush. I would look for places in our house to get a little peace and quiet, just a moment to myself. I'd bathe every night and lock the door just to escape the noise and chaos. Not anymore. Not now. Not since the divorce. I would give *anything* for it all back. The laughter and screaming, the silly sounds and the "busy." I hate the quiet now on the weeks they are at their dad's house. I hate how I can hear myself breathe and every sound in the house. I go upstairs sometimes and lay in their beds. I wonder what they are doing and if they are okay without me.

… I know, pathetic. But I miss the noise. I never ever expected to hate the quiet so damn much.

Safe kisses. When your kids are with you all the time, you take the little shit for granted, like kissing them goodnight or tucking them into bed. When Mark and I were married, I would dread it—the nighttime routine was so annoying! The bath or shower, the book, and the song. The struggle, the fight … no one ever wanting to go to sleep without one last kiss. One. More. Kiss.

Now, when the boys are at my house, I kiss them every night (yes, even at fifteen and sixteen). I still go upstairs, even if I'm writing or busy, and I get in their faces, and I kiss them up. Why? Because I only have them half of their lives. And I no longer get to kiss them every single night like I used to.

Shit, friends! Why didn't you tell me?

Woulda. Coulda. Shoulda. ;)

---

[1] http://www.prestonwoodchristian.org/uploaded/Parent_Pages_-_Sex_and_Dating.pdf

Just the TWO of Us

You used to be a family.
Just one family.
Now you are a family—divided.

There are two houses, with two different addresses … and maybe even two different zip codes. In those houses, there are two sets of clothes for each kid, two toothbrushes, and, if they are lucky, two rooms that they get to decorate differently at each house. At my home, Jonah did basketball, and Zac did Tigers baseball. At Mark's, it's the Steelers for Jay, and Michigan Football for Zee. (They think that's pretty fucking cool, thank the lord. We did something right! Phew.)

Usually, there is some stuff that goes back and forth between the two houses each week, like backpacks for school, books they need for class, and their favorite items. But everything else we have asked for doubles of, not kidding. We even got two retainers made for Jonah after he got his braces off, and I got an extra prescription for Zac's asthma meds just so we could avoid driving back and forth if they ever forgot something.

Mark and I used to be closer in proximity when we first got divorced; now we are twenty minutes apart. You wouldn't think that's a big deal! But in rush hour traffic on a weeknight, or if one of them forgets a paper for school or their iPad, it's a shit show. An hour there and back and nobody's happy. Nobody! So, it's doubles of everything. Two thousand pairs of underwear, a million socks, and tons of shorts. Twice the number of shoes, hair products, and shampoo. We just do it out of mere convenience. Anything we can do to make it less stressful for them and more accessible for us, it is worth it.

Now ... here is where it gets tricky.

When Zac was in the fourth grade, his teacher asked him *which parent* was getting the holiday gift they were making in class that week. In front of his whole damn class. Zac fucking freaked. We had just gotten separated and he didn't even want to talk about it with us, let alone his friends at school. He started to cry and ran out of the classroom. I got phone calls from almost half the moms from his class that afternoon, asking about our divorce. I almost killed his teacher and went to school the next day with guns blazing. Really? *Who gets the fucking holiday gift you're making in class, you dumb bitch? How about you MAKE TWO?* One for each house! Well, apparently that is what she did, and Zee was okay with that. One macaroni picture frame for Dad's house, and one for mine. Poor fella. My heart was broken for him.

And then there's the stigma
of being "divorced parents."

At back-to-school night the teacher asks, "Who are Zac's parents?" and we raise our hands—from two different sides of the classroom. Then the teacher says, "Oh, divorced! Okay!" Like she will make a note of it, and if he's having trouble during the year, she will know why or something. What the fuck? Maybe it's my paranoia, but I can't help it. The stigma is real, isn't it? Or is it not?

I used to think everything horrible that happened in my life was caused by the divorce and being a "divorced parent." But, in reality, that wasn't the case. I came to realize over time that sometimes shit just happens no matter who you are or aren't married to. And no, not everyone was looking at me weirdly or talking about what happened with my marriage. I was just "uncoupled" in a world of happy (or unhappy) couples.

I had to get used to being a "party of one."

… Until a couple of years ago, when I met another party of one. We have since become a party of two—ha—and my life has slowly started to look up. Not that I had to have a man to be happy. That is not what I'm implying, but it sure does make doing "couply things" way more fun. I have a date for school functions … and I don't have to sit at the "Flying Solo" table.

Ummm … yah. That was actually a thing: The Flying Solo Table at my kids' school auction. I almost left that night to throw myself off the top of the parking deck. As if being single at a school party wasn't bad enough, the PTA had to actually name the divorced parent table that?

And I have a partner to take to other things, too. Not that I'm invited to much after all, I'm still divorced. But I have a date now! Having a partner is excellent and I don't feel like such a big, fat loser. Plus, having a man around makes me feel a little bit safer at night, and my boys now get to see me in a loving, healthy relationship with tons of kissing and showing of affection. Jim is fun, and funny, and he makes me laugh lots, which makes my kids happy. I can see it on their faces.

And they tell me they are happier knowing I am happy. All of this is a huge relief for me, obviously. I mean, after all, I want them to feel comfortable around the man I love, and it's a weight lifted off my shoulders that they approve of the new person in my life.

I waited a long, long time to introduce Jim to the kids after having made the mistake of doing it way too early with past boyfriends. I made sure he was in it for the long haul, and we both agreed it was an appropriate time. It was important for the boys to see how well he treats me, and how much I love him. Jim and I still have two houses, and he has his kids and his ex … oy. Two houses, four kids, two exes, and a whole lot of life ahead of us to figure out. But we are both just living in the moment.

Just the two of us, taking it one day at a time. ;)

He's got a WHAT?

I have this great guy.
I met him online.
It's been twenty-three months, three days,
one hour, and six minutes.
... But who's counting?

Jim is smart, funny, and everything I've been looking for my entire life. He has met my kids, my friends, and he even went to meet my family in Detroit over Thanksgiving. His toothbrush is at my house, and I have a whole drawer at his (ha). Annnnddd ... I have doubles of most of my essentials over there too. My makeup, face creams, shampoo, even my razor! The best part? We. Are. In. Love!

Sigh.

Life can't get much better.

... Oh, what was that?

Excuse me? Hold the fucking phone. *My* ex-husband was *where?* Ummm ... you must be mistaken! You saw my wasband where and with *whom?*

Oh. My. Gawd. My wasband has a *girlfriend!* I think I might throw up. ... What? That's a perfectly normal reaction, don't you agree? When I hear about my ex-husband out and about with a gorgeous girl, shouldn't I react this way? Like a fucking psychopath; a nut job? I hope my friend who saw them got the bitch's name so I can start my Google search. I must get this chick's name pronto and begin the social media stalking.

Do you think she's smarter than me? Prettier or skinnier? Does she have kids? Where is she from? Will she treat my boys nicely?

(She better fucking treat my boys nicely!)

I knew this was all going to happen one day; I did. I just never thought it would be this soon. It's only been four years since our divorce. How could he get over me so quickly? Did I mean nothing to him? *How could he do this?*

… I must get the dirt on this little hussy. She clearly is a gold digger. She must know how smart and successful he is, she must know he's only the greatest catch in town! I must put a kibosh to this immediately.

I must be out of my mind as I sit here searching Google for my ex's girlfriend at 12 a.m.

Yes! I found her on LinkedIn. That was easier than expected. Dammit all to hell! She is lovely, great smile … and a social worker. Graduated from the University of Michigan, doesn't surprise me one bit. He likes them smart and stuck up. I kid, I kid. (Kinda.) He went there, and that's nice that she did too. How cute. (Barf.) Wow, she has a master's in special education. And look at all the philanthropic organizations she is a part of. (Damn it.) She does look uber-fabulous on paper, lovely on screen. No wonder he likes her; I like her, too. (Mother fucker!)

Okay breathe, Jennifer. All of these feelings are normal, and I'm sure he felt the same way when you brought that dipshit Andy to Jonah's Bar Mitzvah two years ago. Or when he met that loser Steve who ended up being a sociopath. I mean, he was jealous, right?

Well, if he was jealous … he never showed it.

He was calm, relaxed, and totally chill.

He was respectful and gave me space. He was kind to those men and only asked that they be sympathetic to the boys. What is wrong with me? My ex has found what seems to be a pretty amazing woman. And I am dating a kick-ass man too! What the fuck, Jen? But you know this shit never feels right. The first time you see the father of your children in love with another woman—ya know, start to give her attention, put her first—even if you are the first to date, or get serious, it still hurts just the same. How could it not? He is the sperm to my egg. And I will always have a deeper, stronger connection to the man who gave me those babies.

I'm forever attached to him, no matter what, forever and always.

So, I called my man, and told him about Mark's new woman. "Jim! She is perfect, and pretty, and … he is going to marry her; I just know it!" I said, freaking out.

He said, "Jennifer, don't you want that for your boys? A good woman to love them too?"

Fuck. He's so smart. I have the best guy ever. He's so right! Of course I want Mark to be happy. I want him with a beautiful, caring woman, so my boys have another stable relationship to emulate.

> I want Mark to be happy, just like I am happy.
> I want him to be happy so my boys are happy.

But ...

Do I want *her* tucking my boys into bed at night? Talking to them about dating and girls? Saying things I'm not sure I want them to hear? I mean, I won't even know what they're talking about at all. What if she doesn't believe in the same things we do regarding religion, values, or ethics? These are big topics I've tried to teach my kids. I know this is a new relationship, but there are so many "what-ifs," and I have *no* control over any of it. I can't tell her how to dress or act around them. Oh crap, what if she has kids too, and they are assholes?

OMG! My head is spinning.

I keep spinning and overthinking. It's what I do best, honestly. I think it's a chick thing. Jim says I'm the Queen of Overthinking, but I know these are all "junk thoughts," and I wish I could stop them from taking over my brain.

Now that I think about it, I have no clue if Mark likes her enough to introduce her to our kids, or how long he's even been with her at this point. *Breathe, girl.* And I have to trust him too. He is a good dad and would never pick a woman (or take her around our boys) who wasn't up to par.

After all, he has fantastic taste.

He chose me, and I am pretty flippin' outstanding.

I will just wait patiently and meet this lady before I lose my shit. I'll let it all play out and hope for the best. Who knows? Maybe my boys will absolutely love her. Maybe Mark will call me up and tell me he has found the girl of his dreams. And maybe I will get to help plan a wedding that is *not* mine. (Ha.) And I can be a guest and wear a hot little black dress.

Fuck yes.

... Oh, hold on. My girlfriend just texted. What? You heard *what?* They BROKE UP ALREADY? OMG! Well that was fast. I wonder what happened. Well, she *did* graduate from University of Michigan, that bitch. C'mon, Mark. You've gotta date a girl who went to Michigan State. ;)

Money Honey

I had the most beautiful house.
On the most beautiful street.
In the most beautiful part of town.

We had a beautiful yard, with beautiful trees, and gorgeous flowers. Everything was so beautiful. Even my backyard was pretty. Shit. My life was so fucking pretty I could puke. I had the cars, and the house, and the squishiest little French bulldogs. We lived across from the most prestigious golf club in all of Charlotte. I mean, life was pretty perfect. At least, it all *looked* perfect from the outside; the inside was not. Just like many of our friends, however, Mark and I faked it well. Facebook helped us look even better. And as time went on, the facade cracked away and I just couldn't do "fake" any longer.

Glass. Houses. Shatter.

We got our divorce and promised to be amicable; it had to be amicable for the kids, or I wasn't going to do it. I told Mark if we couldn't be nice to each other and use a mediator, then fuck it. He'd be stuck with my bitchy ass forever! I meant it. Every single word. And we did use a mediator so we didn't give some asshole attorney our money. Then we did our own settlement, which saved time and a boatload of money. It all went pretty smoothly. We agreed, for the most part, on everything. It was as seamless as it could have been.

It was only then when I realized my entire life was about to change. See, I was a SAHM. I'd never even balanced a checkbook.

Whooooaaa ... Now stop here for one minute. Rewind to fifteen years before my divorce, the week Mark met me. I was a) living on my own in a rental house in Birmingham, Michigan, paying all my own bills, and, yes, balancing my own checkbook; 2) working at a kick-ass entertainment company as a DJ and making a great living; 3) supporting myself; and 4) completely independent from Mommy and Daddy.

What the hell happened to that woman?

During my twelve-year marriage, I had never seen a bill or a credit card statement. I never even so much as went to the bank to take out cash ... I mean, why would I have? I was at home all day with the boys, and when I needed money, I just used my debit card. So what, right? I had money, and I spent it when I wanted to spend it. I would online shop and go to the mall. I'd do pretty much whatever I wanted and when I "spent too much," I would get yelled at! Okay, not really yelled at, a slap on the hand, and then I'd be back online at Nordstrom shopping again. I mean, isn't that how it works in most households? Yah?

... No? Ummm, great. (Not.) I had no idea how much money we had when it came time to split it all fifty-fifty. I had been out of my career and raising my babies for so long, I didn't even think about money. In fact, I was married to an accountant, why would I even bother? Does this sound at all familiar? Keep on reading ....

I had no idea where the money was kept. I had no idea
how it was kept. Bonds, stocks, IRAs … retirement,
trusts, 401Ks … fuck! It was all Greek to me!

I was a fucking dumbass and I had no clue what to ask, what to look for, or who was supposed to give me what. And thank you sweet baby Jesus I have a *good* ex, because he was honest and did me right. Many men do not. Let me say that louder for the back of the room, ladies.

Many men do not do right by their ex-wives! Period. And many women have no clue where the money is, just like I didn't.

Many men would look at a woman who was in my position and take full advantage of her. I was stupid and naïve. Girls, if you ever have to split your assets, you better know full on what you're doing, or you will be fucked over twice on Sunday.

Regardless of whether you and your spouse wind up together or apart, you need to be prepared. Married or not, you should fully understand your finances and prepare yourself for any unexpected life change. Prepare yourself for being raked over the coals financially, and you will avoid so much extra stress and anxiety. Get your boats in a row now and it will be smooth sailing should it ever come to that.

Jen's Simple Tips for Financial Literacy

1. Get all your paperwork together.
- Checking and savings account statements (past year)
- Retirement account statements (current, if contributions haven't changed)
- Investment account statements (past year)
- Ledgers for any loans, including your mortgage, auto loans, and personal loans (past year)
- Credit card statements (past year)
- Recent pay stubs if applicable
- Lists of assets and debts brought into the marriage and those accumulated since marriage
- Income tax returns (past three years)

2. Call an attorney, even if you don't plan on hiring one. You need to be prepared for resistance. Even if you decide to use a mediator moving forward, things might get a bit more heated or argumentative and an attorney may be imminent. And you will need an attorney to file your court documents anyway. Again, it's all about being prepared.

3. Open your own checking/banking account.

4. Change your will and health care proxy.

5. Track your expenses.
- Check your account statements.
- Categorize your expenses.
- Keep tracking consistent (Download an app for tracking or a budget app).
- Build a new budget for your immediate future.

6. Get the correct advice. Divorce laws vary by state, so be cautious of advice that seems to be a one-size-fits-all solution, whether you read it online or received it from a friend. If you're unsure whether you should move money, change accounts, or make any other financial moves pre-divorce, consult with an attorney licensed in your state.

I was fully unprepared for all the drastic changes in my life, but my lifestyle changes were perhaps the most shocking.

I knew I would take a "hit" financially, sure, but I didn't think I'd have to give up the things I was accustomed to. Does that sound obnoxious? I bet. But how about things like health insurance? Or not being able to pay for my migraine medication, or my birth control? How about not knowing if I could pay the rent on certain months? I suddenly needed money for stupid shit I'd never even thought of: water bill, gas bill, cable bill, gas in my car, groceries to feed my kids … ya know, stupid shit? Now I had to pay for *everything* on my own. You name it, I was responsible for it. If a tree fell on my house? Yup. If I needed the toilet fixed? Me! How about an oil change? Or getting the damn grass cut? Y'all, I was clueless. The monthly bills added up quickly, and alimony and child support goes fast.

I had never worried about where my money came from before, or how I was going to live on a daily basis. Surprised? Well, stop right there and smell *The War of the Roses*.

So, I turned in the Land Rover for a Yukon, then realized I still could in no way afford that, so I got an Acadia. I drove it for a year, then figured out a Jeep Cherokee would be more than efficient. Now, this all sounds pretty fucking sickening to some of you, right? *What kind of spoiled princess was this woman?* Well, it is what it is, folks. Some of you may think it's vile; others probably feel my pain. And a few of you are most likely sitting there thinking, "That will never be me. I am never leaving my marriage or this lifestyle." Well, trust me, this shit ain't easy and you do not want to go there!

If you think nothing is worth staying for, then you are probably right … and you should get out of that marriage. (Money can't and never will buy happiness.) But if you think your lifestyle will remain the same as what you had when you were married, you are dead fucking wrong.

Staying home and giving up my full-time career allowed my (ex-) husband to get where he is now, and make the money he's now making. And I worked just as hard taking care of our two babies as he did climbing the corporate ladder. Raising two kids is a full-time job; it's one I'm proud of and will never apologize for.

My ex would have never been where he is
right now in his career without me.

I got what I deserved in my settlement, and it was fair. I didn't ask for anything more than I should have. Now, some women will argue that it's worth the "pay-cut" to get out of a shitty marriage. Okay, if it comes down to that and you feel like giving him everything and just walking out, go ahead.

… But I will think you're a fucking fool!

Look, every state is different; laws are laws. But you deserve what is rightfully yours. Don't "give it up" to avoid an argument or because you "just want to get out." Life is hard enough as a single mom, why make it tougher on yourself and your kids? Get what is rightfully yours so you can give your kids the life they *should* have. Take the time you need to make arrangements and get your finances in order. If you don't have to get out quickly because you're in a dangerous situation, take your time and organize yourself; hire an attorney and financial planner to explain what actions you need to take moving forward so you are prepared.

Don't give away what's yours just to "get out" faster!

My divorce knocked me down a few rungs, sure.

There's no more going into Target and buying whatever the fuck I want. Now I think before I put things in my basket and I return the stuff I don't need. Yes, I actually return it. I had to get a job that pays (I know, right?) and I'm hustling hard AF to make my kids proud of me. I'm trying my best to do this all on my own. I use the giant scroll of coupons from CVS and I try not to eat out excessively. And believe it or not, I had to change hair stylists because I couldn't afford to spend $385 on my fucking hair! (… I know, right?) I don't get my nails done at the fancy place and I can't travel like I used to. Are my boys affected by my change in income? Yes. Do they feel like they got the shaft? I'm sure. Do I think they will be better off for it in the end?

HELL YES.

We live in a world of entitled parents who raise entitled kids. It's a shame mine had to learn the value of a dollar the hard way, but I'm glad they did. I'm happy they can't get the latest iPhone "just because" or the hottest pair of Jordans. I'm not upset I can't take them to Hawaii and stay at the Ritz … and have to get an Airbnb down the strip instead. They are just fine "slumming it." (Ha.) And trust me, they have learned it's just as fun to go with Mom to Wrightsville Beach and stay at the not-so-hot hotel as it is to go with "Fun-Dad" to the most expensive resort in Fiji. Hell, some kids don't get to go on vacation at all, and I know this. And I get it. But it's all relative and I'm sharing *my* story. It might sound obnoxious to some of you, but it's my truth. Don't judge!

> The point is, divorce will change your lifestyle
> no matter what it looks like to begin with;
> just prepare yourself for the hit.

I still feel sad when I can't do the shit my married friends are doing. But I feel more sorry my boys aren't included because I can't afford it. It's not their fault, it's Mark's and mine. They shouldn't be punished for our divorce. Still, the damn guilt never goes away. I still get choked up when I see a gorgeous house that I know "could've been" mine. And I feel even more upset knowing my kids are living in two little houses where they have to go back and forth while Mark and I stay put. (And no, it's not the size of the houses … it's the fact they have to go back and forth.) It just sucks, and it hardly seems fair. They are such troopers; why did we do this to them?

Guilty, party of one!

I still want the yummy shoes, and the fancy bracelets. I'd be lying if I said I don't miss traveling and going away to cool places. I want the boys to experience fantastic things, but unfortunately "fantastic things" come with a high price tag. I want them to have it all, of course. But I also want them to be good, solid humans. I would like them to appreciate what they have and give back to those who have less than us. Most of all, I want them to know they have two parents who are better separated than together, and that we love them no matter where we live or how much money we have. And truly, they want for nothing and ask for nothing.

They are pretty amazing kids if I do say so myself.

I am still sad sometimes when I think about the things we could be doing as a family. We were so good as a team, the four of us together. It was the pair of us, Mark and I, who sucked so badly.

But it's only money, honey, I keep telling myself.

It's only money, Jennifer.

Shaken Families

Ohhh ... my bad.
I meant "blended" families!

Why anyone would call the shit show of "mushing up" two families after a divorce "blending," I have zero idea. There is nothing "blendable" about it! And trust me when I say there is not one person who genuinely wants to be in a blended family. No. There. Is. Not. Not me, not you, and not the children. Hell, even the dog is shaking in his boots.

Here's the sad truth:

There is no such thing as "Happy Blended Family."

Okay, my bad. *The Brady Bunch!* That was the *only* blended family I have ever seen that was perpetually happy ... until Greg and Carol started having sex, then it all went to shit. Haha. But really, people, avoiding the insanity called "blending" is one of the *biggest* reasons (IMO) to stay married. I wish I were kidding, and I wish there weren't like a million stats and horror stories to help prove my case.

And yes, there are always exceptions to the rules. And sure, there are certainly those of you out there (including my editor) who grew up in a healthy, happy blended family. But for the most part (and many therapists and Blended Family Survivors would concur) it's a fucking shit-show. But if you have children, you are tossing around the idea of splitting, and you also think you might one day want to shack up with a new partner ... HOLD 'dem horsies!

Imagine this:

Ready? Let's just say for shits and giggles you, Married Person, are now divorced. *Poof!* Oh, sorry! I know, I just ended your marriage for you. But wait, there's more! I've given you a hot boyfriend (or girlfriend) and he has two awesome little girls! You are so *in love* and things are moving along swimmingly. He thinks you're fab and he loves your three girls too. He has the cutest little dog and lives on the lake, but you live in the city, an hour away. *Rats.* Not the best of scenarios, but you have been dating for a year and it's time to BLEND FAMILIES. Yay! (Not.)

In Mr. McPerfect's opinion y'all should move into his house, 'cause it's bigger. Ugh, but okay. The girls will be fine, you hope. Oh, of course they'll be fine! Kids are totally resilient, and they will adjust. 1) because they have zero choice, and 2) because they have zero choice. (Can you feel the sarcasm dripping off the page?) But sure, I do get it! I do, I'm not totally heartless here. I understand. Remember, I have been in your (hypothetical) shoes! After living apart and commuting an hour both ways for over a year, you two love-birds want to live under the same roof and sleep together every night, right?

But did you ever ask your kids what they want?

No? Oh, silly me. They have no say; this isn't about them, right? Wrong! Did they ask for a stepdad, or a set of new siblings, grandparents, and extended family who they don't even know or give two shits about? No, and they didn't ask for you and their father to divorce either, now did they? And what about the new traditions and rules? Does it seem fair to expect them to just acclimate and adjust after spending their whole lives a certain way?

Your kids didn't ask for you to move into another household with a new family. And they certainly didn't expect to lose quality time and your attention to the extra kids you just added into the mix. And have you considered the fact that they will have to accept this new man as a "father-figure" and his daughters as your new children?

So, let's take a big, deep breath and think before we go shaking up their lives again, shall we?

Now let's consider what happens if and when you decide it's just not working and split up? *Whoooaaa, nelly!* What then? Your girls have just gone through losing a dad (in the divorce), and now they are faced with another "loss" of not only a new guy (who they hopefully like), but his three daughters, too? What a fucking mess!

Blending families is one of the most challenging parts of starting a new relationship after a divorce. And here are some miserable stats: according to the Stepfamily Foundation, approximately forty-one percent of first marriages end in divorce, with second marriage separation rates jumping to sixty percent. Now, if there are children involved (from a previous marriage), the numbers get even higher. If both partners have kids, the odds are stacked against you. SEVENTY percent of blended marriages end in divorce. Unfortunately, blended (or stepfamilies) do not just merge as seamlessly as most would like to believe. It is a far more complicated process than some can even admit. That's because many couples want it to work so badly, they will sacrifice the well-being of their children. They come into the new relationship and family with false expectations, which causes problems from the beginning.

Studies show that stepfamilies who go into this new life with a fairytale, traditional-family approach are destined to fail.

I can remember when I first got divorced and decided to jump right into a relationship with a man who wanted to blend immediately. Our kids went to school together and "kind of" knew each other from being around campus, but not really. He had me convinced that it would be fine for us all to meet and hang out. My kids were fresh out of our divorce and in no way ready to meet him, let alone his two boys, but he was four years post-divorce, and his boys had met many of his girlfriends. We were in entirely different situations, and I was afraid of losing him if I didn't agree to his wants. Ummm, hello!

First mistake: not listening to my gut.
Second mistake: being afraid to stand up for myself.
Third mistake: putting anyone else before my own children.

Now, I knew what I was doing wrong, but when we are in the throes of "true love" and wanting it to work so badly, well, we all just make bad choices. (See all of the above.) Duh. I digress …. My kids met his kids. Weird, awkward, awful. He spent time with my boys—so strange! He was a constant reminder that their dad was out of the picture and it showed on their faces every time that man walked into the room. Then I went on vacation with him and his kids—crazy AF. I loved them so much, bonded with them, and still miss them to this day. I think about them, what they're doing, if they are okay. I know, nuts, right? But I just have this thing:

I can easily love other people's kids like my own; many people cannot.

This man could not love my boys. And neither could the next guy I dated. He broke up with me because I wouldn't have *his* kid; mine weren't enough, he wanted his own. I feel I am different than most, I can love other people's kids. I mean, can you? I'm only asking because so many of my clients and friends (both divorced and married) have answered with a resounding "no." So, ask yourself, can you really? I mean honestly, do you think you could take another child's side in a fight against your own? Or kiss them to bed every night? I have many times, and I would over and over again, but many people are just not physically and emotionally wired that way. And that disconnect can (and will) undoubtedly affect the entire household.

For example: I used to date a man with two little girls. Those girls fell in love with me quickly; and I them. We spent lots of quality time together, much more than I had ever spent with other children of men I dated. Our bond was strong, and I miss them even now, *years* later. Suffice it to say, their dad has since gotten engaged to the woman he cheated on me with, and a couple months ago I ran into the girls at a restaurant for the first time since the break-up. Are you following this? Those girls and I never had any closure, no chance to say goodbye. Their dad and I ended things abruptly and on obviously horrible terms.

The girls saw me from the doorway of the restaurant, both old enough now to make their own decisions, and they ran toward me. Jim and I were at the bar, waiting to be seated. They both grabbed ahold of me, hugging me and crying, "We miss you so much, Miss Jen! Where have you been?" I was stunned, holding back tears. I tried so hard not to cry, but oh my G-d! I couldn't even believe it. I held them both so tightly and the oldest said, "OMG, Miss Jen, we hate Daddy's new girlfriend. She won't even kiss us goodnight before bed."

Y'all. I can't make this shit up. My heart sank and I looked up and she was standing there with my ex. Jim was so cool, he shook the guy's hand as I gathered my thoughts and said, "Hi, you must be, Tracey. I'm Jen."

She pulled the girls away and said, "I know exactly who you are." Then she turned and left. It was the last I saw of them. I still get a lump in my throat thinking about that night. Those poor babies, having to be in a house with a woman like that. They deserve better.

Loving another man's children as your own is harder than you think. And expecting him to bond with your own kids immediately is asinine. Even if you go in with the lowest of expectations, they will still be too high.

When you become a stepparent, you must instantly parent children who are uncomfortable and unfamiliar to you; and you to them. They are expected to be kind and loving when they do not love you—and why should they? They have a mom or a dad; you are just a temporary replacement until they get to the real one. And why would you want this stress for your own kids?

Remember when you were little and you would sleep over at a friend's house and get up and have breakfast the next day? There was always that weird sort of feeling like you were out of place, but you were welcome. Yah! Imagine that … for a really long time.

Look, there are positives to blending families; I'm sure they're in there somewhere if I dig hard enough. There's some website somewhere with a happy couple who actually succeeded at this and got a book published. Or some woman who made a career out of helping people blend families successfully. But if you go on BluntMoms.com (best site ever!), ScaryMommy.com, or any other hot, cool mommy blog, you'll find hundreds of articles on how hard it is to make it happen. There are tricks out there and helpful pointers to being more successful, sure!

But in my opinion, just give your kids the gift
of personal space and your attention.

… Especially if they are older and almost out of the house, or headed off to college in a few years. Let them have the last few years of just you. My ex and I made a pact that neither of us would live with or get married to anyone before our boys left for school. It may sound stupid to some of you, but we are giving our boys (fifteen and sixteen) the gift of our attention. For fuck's sake, after they leave for college, I will be free to do whatever the hell I want! Why would I ruin the stable environment I have made for them during their already stressful high school years by selfishly adding in a new "dad"? Or kids they have to pretend to like?

Haven't your kids been through enough?

I'm not saying don't date or fall in love. I am in a great relationship, and we live an hour apart. Jim and I made a promise to ourselves and our respective kids that blending families would never be in the cards. We each have fifty-fifty custody, and that allows us to have a week on/week off with our kids. We are on the exact same schedule so we can be together for a week, and then with our kids the next. Is it perfect? Fuck no! Is it difficult to go a full week without seeing each other? Ummmm, yes! But we always manage (even an hour away) to find the time. Sometimes we get lunch during the week (while the kids are in school). Or because Jim's kids are a bit younger, I will sometimes leave mine alone for a night and meet him for dinner (or if we have a special event) on a kid week. But usually, the kid weeks are for our kids. Isn't that the point after all?

What would be the benefit of blending?
Yah, nada.

It's not exactly perfect; however, we get to give our kids the attention they deserve for the time we have them. And trust me, we text a ton. And when they go to bed at night, we talk on the phone. We've made it work because we love each other that much. But, we love our *kids* more. And we think they've been through enough. Now, some might argue we deserve to be happy as well and that what we are doing is stupid. And while I appreciate that, I have seen the disastrous stepfamilies some of my friends have created (and left behind), and I'm just not willing to lose Jim or destroy my children.

> I see it as a win-win. I get a full week with
> Jim and then a full week with my boys.
> Both get my undivided attention and love.

And, truth be told, Jonah leaves for college in three years, Zac in four. If Jim and I can't make it that long in two separate houses, then we would inevitably implode in one all together.

Now that I've said my part, here are a few really great tips I've found that I think would be beneficial if you decided not to listen to me and mush your families. I am not so naïve that I don't realize some of you think I'm full of shit, and that blending is fantastic and easy as Sunday morning. So, here you go. (And look, I know most of you will *never* even need these tips. After all, you've obviously been reading along and taking notes on how to stay married. But, in the event that a divorce is in your future, here are some useful tips for blending, you rebel, you.)

TIPS FOR "BLENDED" FAMILIES.

I did some research on some of my favorite mommy blogging sites and I've borrowed some tips I really think are excellent. I also added a few of my own. Good luck, and *may the force be with you!*

Don't ever talk shit about the biological parent. Okay, this seems pretty self-explanatory, but for those of you who need a little help ... do not talk smack about the kiddos' real mom. For fuck's sake! I know you will want to, trust me. I have wanted to say a bazillion horrific things in my day, but no one wins in that situation. The kid will be upset and rat you out. Your hubby will get yelled at, and you will be in the dog house. Note to self: Bite. Your. Tongue.

Family Meal. Ahhhh, do you cook? Yah, me neither! But let's order from Uber Eats and serve it up family style, ya dig? It's uber (ha) important that you all sit around a table and eat together like a family unit. As one, big happy bunch. It's really important to all spend time connecting and forming a bond. Dinner is a spot sans the cell phones where you can all make eye contact and talk about your days. Can you say, "Marsha, Marsha, Marsha"?

Love them ALL. Let's not pick favorites, even if the favorite is yours. (By a landslide!) Act as if you like his too. Even if you can barely stand them ... try. And then, try harder. You do want this to work, right? Then dig deep and like them! Don't always take your kids' side, don't pick yours first for every game, and don't give your kids the easiest chores and stuff. Even Steven, or this is never going to happen.

Practice what you preach. Never let them see you sweat. Or hear you bitch. Or complain. Or act like you think this is the worst idea y'all have ever had. Preach.

You love this blended family shit, and it's going to work! Positivity breeds positive kids. You wanted this, now act like it. Preach!

One on one dates matter. Monday it's you and your kid, Tuesday it's his kid. You go to Ben and Jerry's for your date with his; so pick another spot for yours. Simple enough it seems. Just spend time with each kid separately and don't talk about issues in the house or with the other parent. Try and get to know each other and learn new things.

Daddy knows best. This is not your first time at the rodeo, we get it. But it is your first time trying not to reprimand someone else's child. Whoooo, Nelly! Pull back on the reigns and ease up. He is not your child, so it's not your job to set rules and enforce them ... yet. Until y'all have established who is in charge in the household, it's all him for his kids and you for yours. (At least until you have a sit-down to say otherwise.)

Don't try to be a better mom. We know you're a much better mom than his ex. You're cooler too. You're just a better person. But his kids don't think so, not even close. Now, they might like you or tolerate you ... still, I can assure you they do not believe you are better than their own mom. So, please do not try to be, or imply that you are, or I can guarantee they will push back tenfold.

Now, if they do think you're a better mom, or they tell you how much they love you, there is not a damn thing you should do but smile, and say, "No, honey. Your mom is great." Then, leave the room and do an air fist pump. "Yessss!"

Conclusion: The Secret Sauce

I am proud of you.
You are still here, and I've got your wheels turning, huh?
Lots to think about?

Well, I did tell you this wasn't going to be easy … but we have all been there. Every married person has at some point hit a bump in the road of matrimony, and then begun to question themselves or their spouse. We've all contemplated walking out that door, leaving, and starting over to search for something better.

I was there; I get it.

I am a divorce coach who truly believes that if you can stay married, you should. However, if you have to get divorced, try to do it right—with compassion, and respect for one another. Put your egos aside and those kids *first*.

Remember: do not stay in a marriage that is destructive, or unhealthy. Do not stay for your children if you're not capable of displaying positive and loving behavior. Do not stay if you are feeling unloved, unwanted, or disrespected. But if there is a glimmer of hope, any doubt in your mind …

Stop. Breathe. Think.
And then, breathe some more.

Here's a little thought nugget, a take-away if you will. I always thought it was so important to be a great mom or a fantastic dad. But you know what I've learned along the way? It's more about being an amazing *partner*. A supportive, kind, and loving spouse. The kind of mate you want in your corner. A husband who goes to bat for his wife … and at the end of the day, your wife's got your back.

I was a great mom. No, I was the *best* mom, but I was a pretty shitty wife. I loved those boys more than I ever loved Mark, and I thought it was enough—but it wasn't. I didn't give our marriage the respect it deserved. And I almost never put Mark first. And now, looking back, I thought I was doing the right thing; our boys needed me, and they were my job. I think many mothers feel this way, right? Now, I know if I asked Mark, he would say otherwise, he's such a good guy, and he will totally yell at me when he reads this. (Ha.) But I still have so much regret and feel so much sadness.

I asked the boys just yesterday if they were upset about our decision to divorce. They said "absolutely not." I love them both so flippin' much. Zac said, "Mom, you guys made the right choice. You and Dad would never have lasted. Have you heard him snore?" … Dying, for real. I laughed so hard.

Somewhere along the way we lost each other; being a loving wife was also my job, and I forgot that part.

So, what if we could just love our partners like we love our children, unconditionally with no judgement? What if we could put as much time and effort into our relationship with our spouses as we do our kids? And what if we could love our mates with the same level of compassion we show ourselves?

Can you imagine how awesome our marriages could and would be? (That's how awesome our marriages *should* be.)

So, imagine I had a "Secret Sauce"
for a successful and everlasting marriage
... would you want it?

I mean, who wouldn't? And truth be told, I'm pretty sure this is a fool-proof recipe. If you just follow the directions to this simple, three-part mixture, there is no way you'll end up as a Woulda. Coulda. Shoulda. I only wish I'd had a secret sauce like this when I was married, y'all. It's easy as pie. (Well, I think pie is kinda hard to make.) How about PB&J? Yes, easy as PB&J!

HURVITZ'S SECRET RECIPE FOR A SUCCESSFUL AND EVERLASTING MARRIAGE

1. SEX *The number one, most IMPORTANT factor in your marriage.* Look, I'll say it again: If you don't have sex with your spouse, they will find someone who will. (Sorry, it's true). Intimacy is the glue that sticks y'all together! And once you stop having sex and that connection is lost, it's so hard to find each other again. So, keep it up! Just. Do. It. I don't care how, or where, or when. Make a date once a week, pay your wife in shoes. I don't care what it takes. MAKE LOVE LOTS!

2. SILENCE *Talk less; listen more.* Stop talking and start listening! Listen to each other. Be quiet. Be still. And just be. Take the time to connect and be one with each other. Get time away from the noise and actually listen to what the other person is saying. *Shhhh.* Be Silent. Women stop nagging, men stop yelling. Check your tone and volume. And, when all else fails, go to the Peace Table!

CONTINUED ON NEXT PAGE

3. SMILE Find a way to smile at each other every single day. May sound corny AF, but I don't care. Smile, laugh, and be silly. Stop taking yourselves so dang seriously. Life is too short.

Directions: Do number ONE as often as possible. Keep doing number one. Mix it up. Repeat. Do it again. Add in number two. Wait, then repeat Number One. Always do Number three. Keep repeating in any order until combined fully.
Never, ever stop. Ever. ;)

This book was hard to write for so many reasons. (Okay, here come more tears.) It's not ever easy to admit your faults, own your shit, or share something this personal with the world. Actually, it's the scariest thing I've ever done in my lifetime … well, except for writing my first book. You'd think this shit would get easier? Ha! I've been called a hypocrite for saying I believe in staying married. Divorced women have made nasty comments and said I'm not "supporting our tribe." Some people have even said they feel sorry for my boyfriend because I must "really want my Ex back." (Sorry, but no.) After reading this book, I hope you understand my good intentions and my real purpose for writing it … to help save marriages and those struggling with indecision.

I have wanted to quit more times than you can count, but I saw a real purpose in this book. I had to write it.

Yes, I am pro-marriage.

Yes, I believe in doing divorce right.

And yes, I do believe if there is a glimmer of hope left, you should work as hard as fucking possible to salvage your marriage. There is nothing any easier (or better) over on this side of the fence.

Finally, I believe that although divorce is difficult, it does get better with time. And when I think about it, I'm proud of Mark and myself for keeping our promise to each other to be amicable and stay friends. It wasn't easy at times. Funny, our promise was sort of a "divorce vow" we made to one another. And if you ask Mark, he will tell you I'm the best friend he has at this point in his life. And he is still my ICE (In Case of Emergency) on my cell phone. Oh, and my emergency contact on all my medical forms too. He is a wonderful father and my very dear friend.

But no, I can't imagine being married to him again.

And no, I do not want to give up the life I have created for myself. I mean, shit, I'm important in this scenario too. Don't I deserve to be happy? This is not about living with regret, although I do think anyone divorced (with kids) must have a little regret on some level. It's about how you live life fully *now*, in the present. I can't go back; I won't go back. I am finally (after much struggle and heartache) in a healthy relationship and doing so many outstanding things with my life. I took my divorce and turned it into a career! Hell, I wrote a best-selling book, and an award-winning screenplay to boot. I never would have done any of that had I stayed married.

… And I have myself a brand-new best friend, lover, and partner-in-crime who loves me with all my mishegas, zero judgement.

So, who knows? If I'd stayed in my marriage, I'd probably still be going to the club with all my married friends and learning to play bunco. I'd maybe still be wondering if there was something "bigger out there" for me. I'd still be nasty and angry all the time. I'd still want for more. And I'd still put the boys first, Mark second. Maybe I'd even still resent him for all the things he didn't do, and maybe he'd still be mad for all the things I didn't appreciate.

I think in my case, I had to get divorced to see and learn what I did wrong … so I could make it right. … Except then it was too late. Does that make any sense at all? So, I've made it my mission to help others before they make the same mistakes I did.

If only someone had handed me this book years ago before I signed those divorce papers. Would I have done it all differently? Could I have saved my marriage? Should I have changed my mind?

Woulda. Coulda. Shoulda.

I guess I will never know. But that is the way life goes, my friends. There is no going back, only forward. I hope this book provides some insight to those of you who can do it all differently. Yes, you can still save your marriage, or change your mind. You have the Secret Sauce to a Successful and Everlasting Marriage. Now, go on and use it. Before you become a Woulda. Coulda. Shoulda. ;)

Peace, love, and SO much TRUTH.

xo, j

About the Author

Jennifer Hurvitz is known for her no-nonsense approach to dating after divorce. She's a relationship coach, best-selling author, and host of the *Doing Divorce Right* podcast. Happily divorced since 2014, Jennifer lives in Charlotte with her two kick-ass teenage boys. Through her popular blog, *The Truth Hurvitz,* and weekly podcast, Jennifer helps people understand what a happy divorce can look like and how to dip their toes back into the dating world. She loves sharing her insight on how to stay in a successful marriage too! Reach out via jenniferhurvitz.com if you'd like her to speak at your next event.

Follow Jennifer on Instagram, Facebook, Twitter, and LinkedIn. Grab her first book, *One Happy Divorce: Hold the Bulls#!t,* on amazon.com, barnesandnoble.com and warrenpublishing.net.

CPSIA information can be obtained
at www.ICGtesting.com
Printed in the USA
FFHW020811060619
52856755-58416FF